Very Brief Therapeutic Conversations

In *Very Brief Therapeutic Conversations*, Windy Dryden demonstrates the therapeutic value of very brief interventions in counselling, psychotherapy and coaching, using a wide range of techniques and skills to bring this novel approach to life.

The book provides an informative and innovative guide on 'how to do' very brief therapy in 30 minutes or less. The often fascinating and universal problems the volunteers discuss, as well as the goal and guiding principles of this novel therapy, are explored in the first half of this book. Inspired by Ellis's therapeutic 'Friday Night Workshops', transcripts from Dryden's own therapeutic conversations at his 'live sessions' with volunteers form the second half of the book.

Very Brief Therapeutic Conversations is an accessible and entertaining read for all therapists, whether in training or practice, who want to see very clear examples of theory being put into practice.

Windy Dryden is in part-time clinical and consultative practice and is an international authority on Cognitive Behaviour Therapy. He is Emeritus Professor of Psychotherapeutic Studies at Goldsmiths, University of London. He has worked in psychotherapy for more than 40 years and is the author of over 220 books.

Very Brief Therapeutic Conversations

Windy Dryden

LONDON AND NEW YORK

First published 2018
by Routledge
2 Park Square, Milton Park, Abingdon, Oxon OX14 4RN

and by Routledge
711 Third Avenue, New York, NY 10017

Routledge is an imprint of the Taylor & Francis Group, an informa business

British Library Cataloguing in Publication Data
A catalogue record for this book is available from the British Library

Library of Congress Cataloging in Publication Data
Names: Dryden, Windy, author.
Title: Very brief therapeutic conversations / Windy Dryden.
Description: Milton Park, Abingdon, Oxon ; New York, NY :
Routledge, 2018. | Includes bibliographical references.
Identifiers: LCCN 2017055438 | ISBN 9781138477339 (hbk) |
ISBN 9781138477360 (paperback) | ISBN 9781138477360 (hardback) |
ISBN 9781351105002 (master) | ISBN 9781351104999 (web) |
ISBN 9781351104982 (epub) | ISBN 9781351104975 (mobipocket)
Subjects: LCSH: Brief psychotherapy. | Psychotherapist and patient.
Classification: LCC RC480.55 .D79 2018 | DDC 616.89/147–dc23
LC record available at https://lccn.loc.gov/2017055438

ISBN: 978-1-138-47733-9 (hbk)
ISBN: 978-1-138-47736-0 (pbk)
ISBN: 978-1-351-10500-2 (ebk)

Typeset in Times New Roman
by Out of House Publishing

Contents

Foreword

Windy Dryden has been busy. He has had very brief therapeutic conversations with 245 individuals in front of different professional audiences. Eight of the 245 people have agreed to share their stories in this book.

Very Brief Therapeutic Conversations is a remarkable book because the stories of the eight people briefly interviewed *are* remarkable, as is the impact of Windy's brief conversations with them. Based on Albert Ellis's famous Friday Night Workshops conducted in New York, Windy has not met the volunteers before these conversations occur. He spends 12–30 minutes addressing the problems they present and provides his fellow conversationalists a transcript and a recording of their one-off discussion. Follow-up emails, sometimes years later, suggests that these brief conversations have a profound and lasting effect.

Very Brief Therapeutic Conversations can be read in a number of ways: as a fascinating insight into eight people's unique struggles and how a single therapeutic conversation thoughtfully crafted can potentially change their lives; as a practical guide for readers wanting to learn the craft of counselling; and as an accessible insight into the single-session approach to providing therapeutic services. It could also be read as a challenge to traditional ways of providing help to anyone experiencing mental health problems.

Windy's conversations are with real people with real problems, who show enormous courage talking intimately about their struggles in front of an audience. In doing so, everyone concerned is helping to de-mystify and de-stigmatise therapy and possibly reframing the work as matter-of-fact therapeutic conversations. *Very Brief Therapeutic Conversations* helps break down the somewhat artificial boundaries between 'normal people' and 'clients' – convincingly demonstrating that everyone has problems. Students of the helping professions reading this book will get a feel for how an accomplished therapist responds to having limited time by efficiently identifying a focus for change through clarifying how a person wants to be different. The verbatim transcripts interspersed with Windy's reflections and explanations of his motivations demonstrate practical ideas not always taught in universities. These include a mixture of deep listening and the use of gentle interruptions to remain on task, deconstructing generalisations and actively seeking specific details that result in the person interviewed feeling embraced and understood. The early chapters provide sensible ideas for conducting therapeutic conversations that could equally guide therapists more generally.

Instructive themes consistent with the ideas presented for conducting the therapeutic conversations emerge through the intriguing stories of the eight conversationalists, including the therapeutic power of non-judgemental directness, the strength of a non-pathologising focus and the elegance of balancing curious enquiry with education and the sharing of information. The transcripts show how a time-limited endeavour can create "an immediacy about [the] talking," as described by Lily, a volunteer diagnosed with multiple sclerosis who sought an alternative view about how she was responding to her disability in Chapter 12. The conversation with Lily shows that it is not possible to focus on everything in a short time (or a long time, for that matter) and so, after summarising the possibilities, Windy simply asks Lily what she would like to prioritise during their discussion, demonstrating that there can be moments when the complex art of therapy is simple.

Very Brief Therapeutic Conversations also provides an accessible introduction to the single-session therapeutic tradition that Windy has promoted in the UK. Single-session therapy is based on three research findings: (1) that the most common number of therapeutic sessions across most presentations is one, followed by two, followed by three and so on; (2) that the majority of clients who attend only once report this session being sufficient for their needs at the time; and (3) that it is very difficult to accurately predict who will attend only one session and who will attend multiple sessions. Single-session therapists accept these statistics and hence make the most of every encounter and encourage their clients to do the same, knowing it may be their last.

Making the most of the time you have available, especially in therapeutic contexts, leads to approaches that are authentic and client led.
Simply asking a client, "What would you would like to walk away
with at the end of our session or conversation?" is an essential single-
session therapy question and Windy asks a variant of this question
very early on in most of his conversations.

Windy comes from a rational emotive behavioural therapy counselling perspective. I come from a systemic family therapy framework, but the principles of single-session therapy he uses to guide
his conversations are also relevant to how I conduct a session and are
transferable to most therapeutic contexts.

In the Afterword, Windy poses a number of pertinent research
questions, including, "What is the impact on the volunteers reading
the transcript and/or listening to the recording of their conversation?" I must assume it would have a powerful impact; I recall a
family who watched the video of the only session we had together
16 times, addressing a number of their issues themselves as they
watched it together.

After reading *Very Brief Therapeutic Conversations*, I was left
thinking about what Harville Hendrix pointed out: that significant
change may take a long time, but not necessarily require a long time
in formal therapeutic interventions or sessions.

Readers of this book will see for themselves that profound change
can result from very brief conversations. And this in turn may pro-
foundly change readers' practice.

Dr Jeff Young
Director
The Bouverie Centre: Victoria's Family Institute,
La Trobe University, Melbourne, Australia.

Co-editor of the upcoming book, M.F. Hoyt, M. Bobele,
A. Slive, J. Young, & M. Talmon (Eds), *Single-Session
Therapy by Walk-In or Appointment: Clinical, Supervisory,
and Administrative Aspects*. New York: Routledge.

Preface

I have, for a long period, been interested in brief interventions in counselling, psychotherapy and coaching. In the mid-1990s, I developed an 11-session protocol for brief rational emotive behaviour therapy (REBT) (Dryden, 1995). A few years later, I developed a ten-session brief, educational, small-group approach designed to help clients develop self-acceptance. After I retired from my university position in 2015, I decided to explore very brief and single-session interventions in both therapy and coaching (Dryden, 2016, 2017a, 2017b). One of the reasons that I developed this latter interest was due to the work that Albert Ellis did in what was originally known as his 'Friday Night Workshops'. Ellis followed on from the work of Alfred Adler, who would often interview, in public, a parent followed by that person's child who was deemed to have a problem. In June 1965, Ellis developed these public workshops, which were held at the institute that now bears his name in New York on Friday evenings under the heading 'Problems of Everyday Living' (Ellis, 2007).

At these workshops, Ellis interviewed two members of the audience who volunteered to discuss an emotional problem for which they needed help. Ellis would interview the volunteer for about 30 minutes and then invite members of the audience to ask questions of him and the volunteer, as well as to make observations on the therapy session. The volunteer would then be given a recording of the session for their later review. Ellis and Joffe (2002) discovered that the vast majority of volunteers found this a helpful experience and most of them also benefited from the audience comments.

Inspired by Ellis's example, in 2005, I began to demonstrate the way I work in front of an audience with volunteer members of that audience. In addition to being a guest therapist at the Friday Night Workshop event in New York,[1] I have held demonstration sessions in front of a variety of professional audiences that are interested in seeing first-hand the way I practice cognitive behaviour therapy (CBT). As I will presently discuss, I am best known for my contribution to an approach to CBT known as REBT. However, in addition to the principles and practice of REBT, I am informed by: (i) working alliance theory (Bordin, 1979; Dryden, 2006, 2011); (ii) pluralistic perspectives on counselling, psychotherapy and coaching (Cooper & McLeod, 2011; Cooper & Dryden, 2016); and (iii) the growing work that is being done in the field of single-session and walk-in therapy (Hoyt & Talmon, 2014a). In this book, I intend to show how these strands influence my actual work with volunteers in therapeutic conversations that last for 30 minutes or less and that are conducted in front of an audience.

Perhaps unsurprisingly, there is not much literature on what Barber (1990) has called "clinical demonstrations" in workshop settings. Barber (1990) himself has written on his own work of conducting such demonstrations using hypnotherapy. In doing so, he refers to Bloom's (1981) and Talmon et al.'s (1988) suggestions for helpful strategies in these sessions. Please bear these suggestions in mind when reading the book and, in particular, the transcripts in Chapters 7–14.

Bloom (1992) updated his own suggestions (Bloom, 1981) of what might be helpful in creating success in single-session encounters (including the conversations that are the concern of this book) to as follows:

- Identify a focal problem.
- Do not underestimate the patient's strengths.
- Be prudently active.
- Explore then present interpretations tentatively.
- Encourage the expression of affect.
- Use the interview to start a problem-solving process.
- Keep track of time.
- Do not be overambitious.
- Keep factual questions to a minimum.
- Do not be overly concerned about the precipitating event.
- Avoid detours.
- Do not overestimate a client's self-awareness (i.e. do not ignore stating the obvious).
- Help mobilise social supports.
- Educate when clients appear to lack information.

Rosenbaum et al. (1990) and Hoyt and Talmon (2014b) added to Talmon et al.'s (1988) suggestions for useful strategies in single sessions that are again applicable to the very brief therapeutic conversations that are my concern here. These are as follows:

- Expect change.
- View each encounter as a whole, complete in itself.
- Do not rush or try to be brilliant.
- Emphasise abilities and strengths rather than pathology.
- More is not necessarily better. Often less is more.
- Focus on pivot chords.[2]
- Life, not therapy, is the great teacher.
- Big problems do not always require big solutions.
- The essence of therapy is more about helping clients to help themselves than about the therapist's need to be needed.
- Most clients have limited resources and these should be preserved and respected.
- End the session in a way that allows the client to realise useful implications.

I have titled the book *Very Brief Therapeutic Conversations* because it aptly describes the context of the work that I focus on here. I have neither met the volunteers before the conversation nor are likely to meet them after it.[3] All we have is the time at our disposal to have a very brief conversation designed to help the person in some way.

Windy Dryden
London, Eastbourne
August 2017

Notes

1 Since Ellis's death in 2007, this was renamed 'Friday Night Live'.
2 In music, a pivot chord is one that is ambiguous and contains notes common to more than one key. It thus facilitates movement in several directions. In very brief therapy, such pivot chords facilitate healthy reframing.
3 The exception to this is where I have asked several volunteers to comment on our work and what they later made of it for this book. Also, I send the volunteer both a digital voice recording and a transcript of our conversation as soon as the latter is available.

Acknowledgements

First, I wish to thank all 245 people who volunteered to engage in a very brief and hopefully therapeutic conversation with me in front of an audience. I especially want to thank the eight volunteers who gave me permission to include the transcripts of our conversations in the book.

Second, I acknowledge the contribution of Albert Ellis to the development of the way I carry out very brief therapeutic conversations and for pioneering the Friday Night Workshop (now 'Friday Night Live').

Third, I would like to thank my colleagues, Phil Pearl and Nicola Martin, with whom I co-host the United Kingdom Cognitive Behaviour Therapy Meetup group, where I carry out most of my very brief therapeutic conversations. They have given me the opportunity to hone my very brief therapy skills and, without their respective organisational skills and sponsorship, this group would not exist.

Fourth, I would like to thank Georgie Aronin (www.protypeservices.co.uk) for transcribing all my very brief therapeutic conversations and for helping me collate and analyse the data presented and discussed in Chapter 6.

Finally, I want to thank Jane Lessiter, who graciously read and commented on the first draft of the manuscript and made some very helpful observations and suggestions.

Part I

Principles and practice

Chapter 1

The principles that guide my work in very brief therapeutic conversations

Introduction

The focus of this book is on very brief therapeutic conversations (VBTCs) that I have had with people who volunteered to participate in such conversations in front of an audience. In this chapter, I will review, in brief, the principles that guide my work while conducting VBTCs, but before I do so, let me say something about the context of such conversations.

The context of VBTCs

The events that provide the context for such conversations are ones where people have come to see me either: (i) demonstrate the way I practise cognitive behaviour therapy (CBT),[1] or (ii) lecture on a particular psychological topic followed by me carrying out VBTCs with volunteers from the audience who are seeking help from me for a problem relevant to the topic.

When I call for a volunteer from the audience, I ask that the person volunteers only if they meet the following criteria:

1. *They have a genuine, current problem for which they want help.* It is important that the person does not (a) manufacture a problem, (b) roleplay someone else who has the problem (e.g. one of their clients if they are a helping professional) or (c) present a problem that they had in the past that is no longer current. In my view, unless the person has a genuine, current problem and wants help with that problem, then the ensuing conversation is a sham and cannot be described as a VBTC.
2. *They are willing to discuss the problem in front of an audience.* Normally, the audience is exclusively made up of helping

professionals, or it comprises a mix of such professionals and members of the general public who have an interest in CBT/ rational emotive behaviour therapy (REBT) or the specific topic on which I am lecturing. At the outset, I ask members of the audience to observe the confidentiality principle of 'what is said here, stays here' and ask anyone who will not observe it to make themselves known. In the 12 years in which I have conducted VBTCs, nobody has objected to this principle.[2] I then quip that I don't mind them going away and telling people what a lousy therapist I am, but I do mind if they disclose the content of my conversation with the person. I also make it clear that audience members are not allowed to make recordings of the ensuing conversation. I point out that I will make such a recording, which I will send to the volunteer so that they may have a copy of our conversation for later review (see Chapter 5).

Before I begin a conversation, I ask members of the audience to remain very quiet during the interview and to refrain from even whispering to their neighbour, as in the kind of rooms I do this work, even whispers can be heard and be distracting. I remind them that they will have the opportunity to ask questions of the volunteer and me after the conversation has been concluded. With that done, I commence the conversation.

Guiding principles: an overview

In this chapter, I will provide a summary of the principles that guide my work in conducting VBTCs before discussing each of them in greater detail later. The purpose of this chapter is to provide you with an idea of the foundations that underpin this work. Let me stress at the outset that while I make use of some principles in carrying out VBTCs, I certainly do not make use of them all in every VBTC. I utilise certain principles with some volunteers and other principles with others. For example, while I often draw upon certain key REBT principles, sometimes I don't use these principles at all. This is because perhaps the most important principle that guides my work is as follows.

The person is more important than any principle

As I will soon make clear, my goal in these conversations is to help the person take away at least one thing that they can use in their life going forward that will make a difference to them. I will use any idea at my disposal to help them to do this. In doing so, I prioritise the person's interest over any allegiance I have to a valued principle.

One thing

When I began engaging in VBTCs in front of a public audience, I was much more concerned to show members of that audience what a fine therapist I was than I am now. This led me to make a routine error in that I gave volunteers too much to digest in a short period. I call this 'Jewish mother' syndrome. When I used to visit my dear late mother, she would always make sure that I would not go hungry. She would offer me too much food when I was there and gave me more food to take away with me, "just in case." By contrast, my goal is to offer the volunteer one thing that they can digest and act on in their life to make a difference to that life. In VBTCs, 'less is more' (Talmon, 1990).

The effectiveness of VBTCs depends on a fusion between what I bring to the process as therapist and what the volunteer brings to the process

The predominant therapeutic tradition in single-session work is known as the 'constructive therapies' (Hoyt, 1998). This tradition is composed of therapeutic approaches such as narrative therapy (e.g. McLeod, 1997), solution-focused therapy (e.g. Ratner, George & Iveson, 2012), systemic therapy (Hedges, 2005) and strengths-based therapy (Jones-Smith, 2014). The goal of the therapist in these approaches in single-session work is largely facilitative. It is to help the client draw upon and use resources and strengths that they already have and are not using. The expertise of the therapist is in the mobilisation of client resourcefulness and not in offering a particular content-based view of how clients develop problems and how they can best approach these problems.

Hoyt et al. (2018) contrast this 'constructive' approach with an active-directive approach to single-session work. They would say that my approach to VBTC was active-directive "in which change, even if informed by the client's goals, is primarily brought about through the application of therapist techniques...It is the therapist who forms an opinion about what is wrong (e.g. 'How is the client stuck?'), and then it is the therapist who proceeds to provide what the therapist discerns to be the needed remedy – be it insight, explanation and instruction, specific skill training, paradoxical behavioral directives to obviate interpersonal problems, etc." While I agree that my approach to VBTCs is 'active-directive', I disagree with Hoyt et al.'s apparent view that the volunteer is the passive recipient of the therapist's wisdom. My view is that I do have expertise as a therapist that I am willing to share, but the volunteer is an active participant in the process and brings their view of what might be helpful to them, which also informs my work. That is why I say that my approach to VBTC is a fusion of what I bring to the process and what the volunteer brings to the process.

Helping the volunteer to get the most out of our conversation

As noted above, I see one of my tasks as to help the volunteer to get the most out of the VBTC. I do this in three ways. First, I want to discover what the person has already tried to solve their problem. In doing so, I strive to find out what the person has done that has been helpful and what they have tried that has been unhelpful. During our conversation, my goal is to help the person to capitalise on the former and to refrain from using the latter. Second, I want to discover and make use of the volunteer's internal strengths and access to external resources where appropriate during the conversation. Finally, I want to discover and make use of the volunteer's core values to promote emotional problem-solving.

Principles from REBT

I am most closely associated with the approach to CBT known as REBT, and I do draw from this approach some principles that guide my work in VBTCs. This is part of my expertise as a therapist in VBCT, which I discussed above. Amongst others, I am particularly guided by the following principles:

- It is important to face and deal with adversity rather than to avoid it or skirt around it.
- Flexible attitudes tend to promote psychological health, while rigid attitudes tend to promote psychological disturbance.
- The person's response to their initial response to adversity is more important than that initial response.

• Knowing why an attitude is problematic is not an end in itself. It is the beginning of a process.

• Unless a person repeatedly acts on a new healthy attitude, it will remain theoretical, but won't influence emotion or behaviour.

The importance of understanding, emotion and action

Whether I am using an idea that comes from REBT or from some other source, it is important that the volunteer understands the idea, agrees with it and can see its relevance. If not, then the idea will have no value for the person. Having said that, no matter how valuable such an idea is for the person, if they do not have an emotional response to it, then the idea will probably not stay with them for very long. Even if the idea does have emotional resonance for the person, unless they act on the idea, then it will not help them to solve their problem. So, in a relatively short period, I try to promote affect-based understanding in the volunteer and encourage then to make a commitment to act on that understanding. That for me is the gold standard for a VBTC. I recognise that often this does not happen, but as my mother used to say, "If you don't try, you don't get," and who am I to argue with my mother?

Acceptance and change

I am guided by the principles of acceptance and change in my work in VBTCs. Acceptance is often a prelude to change and it is also important if the change is not possible. However, change based on non-acceptance usually is transitory. I will consider the concepts of acceptance and change in greater detail in Chapter 2, where I will carefully define the concept of acceptance, a term that has several different meanings, which may make its use problematic in VBTCs.

The contribution of pluralism

I am influenced by the concept of pluralism in psychotherapy, which, for our purposes here, involves acknowledging that: (a) all approaches to therapy have value; (b) there are multiple pathways to change; and (c) I need to privilege the client's view on how to tackle their problem when this is in conflict with my view. I thus bring a decided pluralistic stance to the CBT/REBT-influenced work I do in VBTCs.

The importance of the working alliance in VBTCs

I have written elsewhere in great detail on the importance of the working alliance in the practice of counselling, psychotherapy and coaching (Dryden, 2006, 2011, 2017c). Although I only have up to 30 minutes with the volunteer, I am still guided by working alliance considerations. In short, the working alliance in VBTCs comprises four interconnected components:

- Bonds – the interconnectedness between myself and my volunteer.
- Views – the various understandings that we have about salient aspects of the process.
- Goals – what we both want to achieve from the conversation.
- Tasks – what we are both prepared to do to help the volunteer achieve their goal.

I will discuss the working alliance in VBTCs more fully in Chapters 2–5.

The therapeutic, educational and entertaining features of VBTCs

I am guided by the realisation that when I conduct a VBTC, I have a threefold purpose. First, and primarily, I have a therapeutic purpose. I am trying to help a volunteer with a genuine personal or interpersonal problem. This problem is usually a painful one for the person and I owe them a duty of care both for how I help them with the problem and for how I manage the setting where they are disclosing personal material in front of an audience. While it is important that they engage their feelings during the conversation, it is also important that they do not lose control unless it is acceptable for them to do so. If I have any concern about this latter issue, I will check with them to see if they wish to continue or not. I have conducted over 250 VBTCs and have yet to have had an experience where a volunteer ended the conversation for this or for any other reason, but it could happen, and again I want to emphasise that the welfare of the volunteer is paramount.

My second purpose is an educational one. It is rare for people to see therapy conducted live and gain a sense of what a therapist does rather than what he, in this case, says he does. So, when I conduct a VBTC, I am mindful of my educational responsibility to the audience members. I am there, in part, to demonstrate how I work. If the event has been advertised as an REBT event, I have some responsibility to the audience to show them how *I* practise REBT. I have emphasised the word 'I' here because there is variation among REBT therapists concerning how they practise REBT (Dryden, 2002). So, the audience is always going to get 'REBT-WD' when they watch me practise REBT. However, if the event has not been advertised as one where I am going to demonstrate a particular approach, then I conduct VBTCs in my way, free from any responsibility to deliver what has been advertised.[3] Just to reiterate, I see my educational responsibility as secondary to my therapeutic responsibility should the two responsibilities conflict.

My final responsibility is not only to educate the audience, but also to entertain them, to some degree. I do this by using humour in my VBTC with the volunteer. I will discuss this use of humour in Chapter 2.

Focus, specificity and, if possible, generalisation

I have underscored the point that a VBTC lasts for about 30 minutes and often less. This means that I need to create a focus with the volunteer and help us both to keep to this focus. This focus will most often be a problem that the person wishes to discuss and a target for change. I will call this the 'target problem' in this book. I will discuss this issue further in Chapter 5. Once I have created a focus, it often helps for us to work with a specific example of the target problem. For reasons that I will explain in Chapter 5, the best example is an anticipated one. While I am working with a specific focus in a VBTC, I am also looking for an opportunity to help the person to generalise their learning, a point that I will again discuss in Chapter 5.

Assessment, not case conceptualization

Although the time that I have with a volunteer is very brief, I spend quite a bit of this time clarifying the problem and assessing it. This involves two stages. First, I endeavour to convey an accurate empathic understanding of how the volunteer sees the problem and from there I use a conceptual framework (usually, but not always, REBT's Situational ABC framework – see Chapters 3 and 5) that they may find useful. I strive to blend the two viewpoints where possible. What I do not have the time to do is to carry out a case conceptualisation linking all of the person's problems together with contributory and maintaining factors. Having said this, I am mindful of these factors and will utilise them when they become salient, but I do this, if at all, as I focus on the target problem. When I do discover such factors, I look for ways to use them in any generalisation suggestions I may make to the volunteer.

There is a view in CBT that one cannot utilise change-based strategies before one has carried out a conceptualisation of the 'case'. I disagree when it comes to VBTCs. I do say, however, that if I were to try to engage a volunteer in a VBTC without carrying out an accurate assessment of the person's target problem, then I would be making a rod for my own therapeutic back!

The goal-directed nature of VBTCs

I often say that very brief work in CBT should preferably be both problem-focused and goal-directed and this is also the case in VBTCs.[4] Being goal-directed is particularly important as if my volunteer and I are not on the same page regarding their goals, then they will not derive as much benefit from the conversation than if we are in agreement on what they want to get out of the process. Agreeing on goals with volunteers is more difficult than it may appear and I will discuss this issue in Chapter 4.

The importance of a 'good enough' ending

Therapists often talk about the importance of endings in counselling and psychotherapy, and I think endings are also important in VBTCs, but in a different way. The ending of an ongoing therapy can involve the client mourning the loss of an important relationship. This tends not to happen in VBTCs since the relationship only came into being about 30 minutes previously. As such, there is insufficient time for this relationship to have become an important one for the person as it may have done in ongoing therapeutic work.

An ideal ending to a VBTC is one where the volunteer has grasped one important point that has the potential to solve their problem and make a difference to their life if they apply it having made a commitment to doing so. This does not always happen, of course, but it is one for which I strive. To paraphrase my dear mother's maxim: "If you do not strive for an ideal ending, you won't achieve it." And I would add the rider, "But striving does not guarantee achieving."

What is more realistic is a 'good enough' ending. This involves the volunteer taking away something of value from the conversation without it necessarily having the potential to solve their problem, at least immediately. However, it may involve them taking a step in the right direction to solving the problem. In this sense, a 'good enough' ending may include the person:

- Gaining relief or some kind of release from discussing their problem in front of an audience.
- Looking at their problem with a different, more helpful perspective.
- Deciding to seek more ongoing help with the problem.
- Realising that the problem was not as great as it had seemed.
- Realising that they had already taken some productive steps to deal with the problem that they had not realised and resolving to capitalise on these steps.
- Acknowledging that they have the strengths and resources to deal with the problem that they did not realise that they had or that they now see the relevance of these existing strengths and resources to addressing the problem.
- Appreciating that they have solved similar problems in the past and can apply similar methods to solve the target problem.

Helping the volunteer to separate the wheat from the chaff in the audience comments

The VBTCs that I am discussing in this book have all taken place in front of an audience. As I have already mentioned, the audience is either an exclusively professional one or one comprising a mixture of professionals and lay members of the public. At the end of the VBTC, I ask members of the audience to ask questions directed to the volunteer or myself or to make comments or observations on the conversation that they have witnessed. I see my role here as to ensure that the volunteer is not given advice that is, in my view, anti-therapeutic or to highlight points made that may be helpful to them going forward.

Many of the suggestions that members of the audience make are practical in nature, and I reinforce that these may be worth trying once the volunteer has solved the emotional problem that they have most often presented. For example, joining a dating agency may be a good suggestion once the person has addressed their anxiety about going on dates.

When professional audience members put forward a different perspective on the problem that I have taken, I suggest that the volunteer gives this perspective serious thought and if I can see a way of blending these two different perspectives, then I will outline this. For example, when an audience member suggests a psychoanalytic explanation of the problem, I state that the person may be correct, but even if they are, the volunteer still has to address the attitudes and behaviours that they are currently bringing to the problem that result in the unwitting perpetuation of the problem.

Having outlined briefly the principles that guide my work in conducting VBTCs, I will discuss in greater detail the important role that the four components of the working alliance has on how I conduct these conversations.

Notes

1 Sometimes when such an event is advertised it states that I will demonstrate CBT and sometimes that I will demonstrate REBT, a specific approach to CBT (Dryden, 2012a). In my view, CBT is a therapy tradition that comprises a number of different specific approaches to CBT (see Dryden, 2012b). My contribution to the therapeutic conversations that I have with volunteers is influenced, in part, by how the event has been advertised, but my main responsibility is to the volunteers in helping them to address their problems.
2 Whether all members of the audience actually observe this principle is another matter.
3 This book outlines how I practise free from the responsibility of showing any particular advertised approach.
4 While it is possible to engage volunteers in a CBT-influenced VBCT while just taking a solution-oriented stance (i.e. without being problem-focused), one cannot do so by just being problem-focused without being solution-orientated.

Chapter 2

The therapeutic bond in VBTCs

One of the four components of the working alliance in VBTCs is the bond between myself and the volunteer. The fact that the person has volunteered shows that they are willing to participate in the process, even though they may be apprehensive about doing so in front of an audience. Some volunteers comment spontaneously when they first take a seat that they are nervous. I make it a point to ask the volunteer to turn their chair towards me in such a way that they can see me and cannot see the audience. This helps them to focus on the conversation. Several mention after the conversation has finished that they forgot that the audience was there after a while.

Keenness to help

One of the most important ingredients of the therapeutic bond that I strive to create with the volunteer is a keenness to help the person. Right from the start, I attempt to show the person that I am devoted to helping them solve their problem and that I will do all I can to help them achieve this. This means that I will help them to create and maintain a problem-solving focus throughout the conversation. In showing my keenness to help, I guard against rushing the person. When I do my best work, I have a relaxed focus, which I refer to as 'being in a Mesut Özil frame of mind'.[1] However, when I feel rushed in my keenness to help, then paradoxically, I fail to help the person. Thus, I try to bring a 'devoted, but not devout' mind-set to helping the volunteer. But, as Lipchik (1994) suggests, I try to 'avoid the rush to be brief'.

Seek first to understand: the role of empathy in VBTCs

Stephen Covey's (1989) fifth habit in his 'The 7 habits of highly effective people' program is 'seek first to understand before you are understood'. I use a modified version of this principle in conducting VBTCs: 'seek first to understand before intervening'. One of the saddest moments of my professional life was watching my mentor, Albert Ellis, in the twilight of his career carrying out VBTCs in a 'Friday Night Workshop' context and providing off-the-peg solutions to volunteers without striving to understand them first. At the height of his powers, his VBTC interventions were always based on empathy, and his work was superb.

Empathy is based on an understanding of how the volunteer sees the problem from their frame of reference, whereas assessment involves taking that same problem using a professional frame of reference to understand it. When I work empathically with a volunteer, at the outset, I am hoping that the person 'feels' that I understand them. In other words, I am hoping to elicit an affective response from the person. Then, I proceed towards assessing the problem (see Chapter 5). For me, empathy and assessment are complementary. If they conflict, I tend to go along with the client's perspective and work within that rather than imposing a professional perspective that they will not accept. However, for me, the fusion between both perspectives provides the foundation for change.

Finally, it is important that my empathy does not validate the person's perspective when it maintains their problem. For example, if a volunteer says that someone makes them angry, I will strive to convey that I understand that this is their perspective (empathy) without conveying that this perspective is accurate (validation).

Acceptance

It is also important that I convey an attitude of acceptance towards the volunteer. By this, I mean that I see them as an ordinary, fallible human being struggling with whatever concern they have brought to the conversation whose worth is not diminished by the problem or enhanced by solving the problem. As I will discuss in Chapter 5, this attitude of acceptance may be used by the person, if relevant, to address their problem and as such it may be applied to self ('unconditional self-acceptance'), others ('unconditional other-acceptance') or life ('unconditional life-acceptance').

If the term 'acceptance' comes up during the conversation that I am having with the volunteer, I will often define it if I am using the term or ask the volunteer to define it if they have used the term. I do this because the term 'acceptance' has several different meanings and it is important that the volunteer and I are using it in the same way; otherwise, problems may ensue. For example, for me, 'accepting' a situation means the following: (i) acknowledging the existence of that situation and that its existence is a result of a number of pre-existing factors; (ii) evaluating it as good or bad and, if it is bad; (iii) trying to change it if it can be changed or adjusting to it if it can't be changed. Thus, in my usage, acceptance is a precursor to change. It does not mean resigning oneself to the situation without trying to change it.

Seeking permission

Given the limited time that we have at our disposal, I have to work quickly without rushing the volunteer, as noted above. I also have to focus on some painful issues and the volunteer may have to face some painful truths in the process. Consequently, I have found it important to ask the volunteer for their permission to venture into what may be difficult areas for them. I have found that in doing so, their agreement lessens their pain and discomfort because they have agreed to allow the conversation to go into such areas.

The same is true for asking the volunteer for permission to interrupt them. This is an important skill if I am to keep the conversation on track with the agreed focus. Here is an example of a typical exchange:

WINDY: Sometimes in our conversation, you may stray off the point. This is understandable and very human, but if you are going to get the most out of our conversation, if this happens, I will need to interrupt you and bring you back to our agreed focus. Can I have your permission to do this?

VOLUNTEER: Of course. I know that I can go off on a tangent so I would welcome that.

WINDY: Great. If I need to do so, I will, but I will be as tactful as possible.

I have demonstrated this point because I have noticed that therapists often have great difficulty in interrupting their clients. They have been trained not to do so and regard interrupting clients as being rude. However, my point is that unless I am prepared to interrupt the volunteer, I am at the whim of their ability to keep to the agreed focus, and if they struggle to do so, I will struggle to do so. My view is that as long as I have asked and gained the volunteer's permission to interrupt them and as long as I do this with sensitivity and tact, then I am not being rude. Indeed, if I don't interrupt them, I am doing them a disservice in that I am not helping them as effectively as I could.

Humour

I mentioned in Chapter 1 that, as well as having a therapeutic role and an educational role in conducting VBTCs, I also have a role as an entertainer, although this is far less important than the other two roles. The use of humour largely achieves the entertaining aspect of my work. There are several functions of my humour in VBTCs: first, I use it to put the volunteer at their ease; second, it helps to involve the audience; and third and most importantly, it helps the volunteer to stand back and take a humorous look at some important aspects of their problematic functioning.[2]

Self-disclosure

When I am discussing a problem for which a volunteer is seeking help within a VBTC setting, an opportunity may present itself for me to disclose personal information to the person. I would only consider doing so when I have struggled with the same issue with which the person is struggling and when I have had success in employing a strategy that the person may also benefit from using. This would be an example of a coping model of therapist self-disclosure where, in effect, I am saying that I have been through what the volunteer is going through, but I helped myself by developing a healthy attitude and/or by behaving constructively.

A coping model of self-disclosure can be contrasted with a mastery model of self-disclosure. This states that I have not experienced the same problem as the volunteer because I have always thought healthily about the issue at hand and acted constructively.

Once I have judged that coping self-disclosure may be helpful to the volunteer, I first ask permission to share the information. If such permission is forthcoming, then I share the information and gauge the person's reaction to it before I ask what, if anything, the person might take from my experience. Such coping self-disclosure has the helpful effect of humanising the therapist and bringing an important sense of equality to the conversation. It encourages the volunteer to believe that if the therapist has struggled but overcome, maybe they themselves can also do so. By contrast, mastery self-disclosure tends to place the volunteer in a one-down position and the therapist as superior to the volunteer, which only serves to discourage the volunteer in the face of their problem.

Coping self-disclosure is one concrete way in which I can show my genuineness as a therapist, one of the core conditions regarded as therapeutic by Carl Rogers (1957).

Being an authentic chameleon

Having just mentioned genuineness, I want to underscore its importance in making the obvious point that as volunteers are different from one another, then I may have to modify my interpersonal style to work with each of them effectively. I will still be me, of course, but I will emphasise an aspect of myself that I think will gel well with the person in front of me. I do have to make a judgement call on this issue quite quickly, and I may get it wrong, but hopefully, I am flexible enough to make appropriate adjustments to my interpersonal style during the conversation I am having with the person. Being interpersonally flexible is something that my dear friend and colleague, the late Arnold Lazarus, used to stress when urging therapists to be 'authentic chameleons' in their relationships with their clients. He suggested that therapists change the 'colour' of their interpersonal style with different clients, but to do so authentically (Lazarus, 1993).

In taking Lazarus's lead, I vary my interpersonal style in VBTCs along several dimensions, such as 'formal–informal', self-disclosing–non self-disclosing' and 'serious–humorous'. Also, I will vary how metaphorical or how literal I am in my language and how quickly I speak.

In the next chapter, I will discuss the component of the working alliance in VBTCs that I have referred to as 'views' (Dryden, 2006, 2011).

Notes

1 Mesut Özil is a German football player who plays as a midfielder for Arsenal. When he plays, he seems to have the time to assess the situation he is in before making a play.
2 I will provide examples of my use of humour in the transcripts of VBTCs that appear in the second part of this book, although it should be noted that it is difficult to convey humour in such a form.

Chapter 3

The importance of shared views in VBTCs

In 2006, I suggested adding a new component to Ed Bordin's (1979) three-component working alliance framework. He had argued that the working alliance was made up of 'bonds' (how well the therapist and client connect with one another), 'goals' (the purpose of therapy meetings) and 'tasks' (what each person has to do to help the client achieve their goals). I suggested adding a fourth component – which I called 'views' – to address the understandings that both therapist and client had of salient features to do with their therapeutic work. In particular, this covers their understandings of why the client had their problem(s) and how this (or these) could be best addressed. It also covers such practical issues as cost, the length and duration of therapy sessions, the length of the therapy itself and confidentiality. In general, shared understandings are a feature of effective therapy, whereas different understandings that cannot be resolved are an ongoing source of tension in the therapy and do not bode well for a good outcome.

Practical issues

The practical issues that pertain to VBTCs are as follows:

- Each conversation is a one-off discussion of the volunteer's presented concern.
- The length of the session is 30 minutes or less.
- All audience members resolve to keep confidential what is discussed by the volunteer: 'What is seen and heard here, remains here'.
- I will provide the volunteer on request, and free of charge, a digital voice recording of our conversation and a written transcript of it

for their later review. Audience members are expressly forbidden to record the conversation.

Each volunteer understands and agrees to these points before the conversation begins so there is no room for disparate views on these practical issues.

There are two main areas with respect to the 'views' component of the alliance that are particularly salient in VBTCs: understandings of the factors that account for the person's selected problem (known as the 'target problem') and understandings of how this problem can be best tackled.

Views on what accounts for the volunteer's target problem

When I begin a VBTC with a volunteer, I normally say something like, "What problem would you like me to help you with today?" In other words, I initially take a problem-focused approach. As I outlined in Chapter 2, my initial stance is to understand the nature of the problem as the person sees it and to express this understanding to them. I strive to convey the attitude of 'correct me if I am getting things wrong' and sometimes I will state this.

I also listen for the person's views concerning the factors that account for the problem. My position on this, of course, is informed by CBT in general and REBT in particular. But at this early point, I am concerned to understand the volunteer's ideas on this issue. If my views and the volunteer's views are compatible, then I proceed and draw upon the client's views as the conversation unfolds. However, if our respective views are incompatible, I will first ask the volunteer if they would like me to give them my perspective on the factors that account for their problem and, if they agree, I will outline my perspective.[1]

My REBT-based perspective on understanding the volunteer's problem

If I need to explain my perspective to the volunteer at this point, I say something like:

> The approach that I practise is based on an old idea attributed to Epictetus, a Roman philosopher, who said that "People are

disturbed not by things, but by the views that they take of them." We have modified this and say that "People are disturbed not by adversities, but by the rigid and extreme attitudes that they hold towards these adversities." Once people have disturbed themselves they then try to get rid of their disturbed feelings in ways that ultimately serve to maintain their problems. Does that make sense to you?

If the person asserts that what I have outlined does make sense to them, I then ask whether they would find it valuable to proceed on the basis of this perspective so that they can learn first-hand its potential to be helpful to them. If the person disagrees with this position or does not want to proceed with the REBT perspective, then I will go along with their view of their problem and use this to help them as best I can. What I will not do is to impose an REBT or a CBT perspective on a volunteer who is not interested in it.

Views on how the volunteer's target problem can be best addressed

Once the person has outlined their perspective on their problem, then I will ask them for their perspective on how their problem can best be addressed. Again, if this perspective complements my own, then I will proceed and make use of their views as the conversation unfolds. However, if their position is at variance with mine or they do not have a view on this matter, I will again ask the volunteer if they would like me to give them my perspective on how they could address their problem and, if they agree, I will outline this.

My REBT-based perspective on addressing the volunteer's problem

If I need to explain my perspective on therapy to the volunteer at this point I say something like:

> I will help you to identify, examine and change the rigid and extreme attitudes that we argue underpin your problem and to develop alternative flexible and non-extreme attitudes. I will also help you to examine the ways you have tried to help yourself that haven't worked and encourage you to develop and practise more effective, longer-lasting strategies. Does that make sense to you?

Again, if the person states that the approach to addressing their problem does make sense to them, I then ask whether they would see how it applies to their problem to determine its potential usefulness. If the person disagrees with this position or does not want to proceed with the REBT approach, then I will again go along with their view of how best to address their problem and I will use this to help them as best I can. Once again, I will avoid foisting an REBT or CBT approach on a disinterested volunteer.

The situational ABC-based perspective on understanding problems and their realistic solutions[2]

For you to understand the rest of the book, you need to understand how I tend to understand psychological problems and what would constitute realistic solutions to these problems. This section is predicated on the idea that I have already introduced in this chapter that I will not use these ideas if it is clear that they have no value for the volunteer.

The situational ABC model of psychological disturbance

In this section, I will present the model of psychological disturbance that I use in my work. This is expressed in a Situational ABC framework (see the left-hand column in Table 3.1).

'Situation'

The 'situation' represents the actual context in which the problem occurred. It includes the place where the volunteer experienced the problem, the time it happened and the people present. This is the case even when the situation is held in the person's mind, as often happens with problems of anxiety.

'A'

I distinguish between something happening (situation) and what the person finds disturbing in that emotional episode (adversity).

'B'

As discussed in Note 2, with respect to psychological disturbance and health, the term 'beliefs' is used in REBT, while I use the term

Table 3.1 The situational ABC framework of psychological disturbance and health that I use in my work

Model of psychological disturbance	Model of psychological health
Situation	**Situation**
A = Adversity	**A = Adversity**
B = Basic Attitudes (rigid and extreme)	**B = Basic Attitudes** (flexible and non-extreme)
• Rigid attitudes (primary)	• Flexible attitudes (primary)
• Secondary extreme attitudes derived from rigid attitudes	• Secondary non-extreme attitudes derived from flexible attitudes
- Awfulising attitudes - Discomfort intolerance attitudes - Devaluation attitudes (of self/others/life)	- Non-awfulising attitudes - Discomfort tolerance attitudes - Unconditional acceptance attitudes (of self/others/life)
C = Consequences	**C = Consequences**
• Unhealthy negative emotion	• Healthy negative emotion
• Unconstructive behaviour	• Constructive behaviour
• Highly distorted and ruminative thinking	• Realistic, balanced and non-ruminative thinking

'basic attitudes' in my work. When they underpin a psychologically disturbed response to adversity, these basic attitudes are deemed to be rigid and extreme. Of the two, rigid attitudes are deemed to be at the core of psychological disturbance, and extreme attitudes are deemed to be derived from these rigid attitudes.

'C'

In the ABC model of psychological disturbance that I use in my work, 'C' stands for consequences. These are emotional (unhealthy negative emotions), behavioural (unconstructive behaviours) and cognitive (highly distorted and ruminative thinking).

The Situational ABC model of psychological health

In this section, I will present the model of a psychologically healthy alternative to the volunteer's problem that I use in my work. This is again expressed in a 'Situational ABC' framework (see the right-hand column in Table 3.1).

'Situation'

As the 'situation' is the same in both the Situational ABC models of psychological health and disturbance, see my comments on the 'situation' in the section above.

'A'

As 'A' is the same in both the Situational ABC models of psychological health and disturbance, see my comments on 'A' in the section above.

'B'

As noted above, with respect to both psychological disturbance and health, I use the term 'basic attitudes' at 'B' in the ABC framework. When they underpin a psychologically healthy response to adversity, these basic attitudes are deemed to be flexible and non-extreme. Of the two, flexible attitudes are deemed to be at the core of psychological health, and non-extreme attitudes are deemed to be derived from these flexible attitudes.

'C'

In the ABC model of psychological health that I use in my work, 'C' stands for consequences. These are emotional (healthy negative emotions), behavioural (constructive behaviours) and cognitive (realistic, balanced and non-ruminative thinking).[3]

In the next chapter, I will consider the third component of the working alliance: the goals of VBTCs.

Notes

1 Perhaps unsurprisingly, given the public setting in which VBTCs take place, I have never had a volunteer say that they were not interested in my perspective.

2 *Attitude versus belief:* REBT uses the term 'belief' to denote a cognitive appraisal of a meaningful event that largely determines the person's psychological response to that event. However, the term 'belief' is problematic in that common conceptions of it are at variance with how the term is used in REBT theory. Thus, the term 'belief' has been defined by the *Oxford Dictionary of Psychology*, 4th edition (Colman, 2015) as "any proposition that is accepted as true on the basis of inconclusive evidence." So, a client may say something like, "I believe that you don't like me," and while they think that they have articulated a belief, this is not actually a belief as the term has been used in REBT, but rather an inference. As we shall see, it is very important to distinguish between an inference at 'A' and an attitude (or belief as used in REBT) at 'B', and anything that helps this distinction to be made routinely is to be welcomed. Because of this ambiguity of the term 'belief', I decided to use the term 'attitude' in my work in that it better describes the cognitive appraisal that is central to understanding psychological disturbance and health. Indeed, a perusal of definitions of the term 'attitude' will reveal that it is closer to the meaning that REBT theorists ascribe to the term 'belief'. For example, Colman (2015) has defined attitude as "an enduring pattern of evaluative responses towards a person, object, or issue." In deciding to use the term 'attitude' rather than the term 'belief', I realised that if I wanted to preserve the letter 'B' I needed to find a word that began with 'B', and thus I decided to employ the term 'basic attitudes' as suggested by Walter Matweychuk (personal communication) when formally describing 'B' in the ABC framework that I use in my work. While not ideal, this term includes 'attitudes' and indicates that they are central or *basic* in that they lie at the *base* of a person's responses to an adversity. Please note that I use the terms 'attitude' and 'basic attitude' interchangeably in this book.

3 I will discuss this more fully in Chapter 4.

Chapter 4

Goals in VBTCs

Introduction

In this chapter, I will discuss the purposive nature of the conversations that I have with volunteers from the audience attending an event where it has been advertised that I will be doing live demonstrations of therapy. As I discussed in Chapter 1, the event may include me first giving a presentation on a particular psychological topic[1] followed by two demonstrations or it may just be an event where I demonstrate how I work. While there is an expectation that a volunteer will discuss a personal problem that fits the theme of the prior presentation (when one is given), this may not necessarily turn out to be the case. My call for volunteers requests that the person brings a genuine problem *that they wish to address effectively.* I have put these words in italics to show the purposive nature of the conversation. While I have a purpose in having the conversation (which I will discuss shortly), I am inviting someone who not only has a genuine problem, but also has a purpose in discussing it. As I put it, they want to address the problem more effectively than they are currently doing.

My goals in VBTCs

It is not common for therapists to demonstrate how they work in front of an audience comprising fellow therapy professionals and trainees or a mixed audience of lay people and professionals. I have a good role model in this respect in that for many years I watched my mentor, Albert Ellis, give such demonstrations at his 'Friday Night Workshop' held at what is now called the 'Albert Ellis Institute'. I latterly gave such demonstrations myself at this workshop (renamed

'Friday Night Live' after Ellis's death) and continue to do so whenever I visit the Albert Ellis Institute in New York. My goals are very similar to what I imagine Ellis's were.

Helping the person

First and foremost, my goal is to help the person. I want the person to be pleased that they volunteered to have a conversation with me and that I have, in some way, made a positive difference to the way that they are going to address the problem. I want them to leave with 'the one thing' that may make that difference. Keller and Papasan (2015), who wrote a book entitled *The One Thing*, quote a Russian proverb that says: 'If you chase two rabbits, you will not catch either one'. This emphasis on 'the one' both guides me in VBTCs and resonates with me. It is not only a reminder to me to focus on *one* volunteer issue or problem and sometimes to work with *one* specific example of this problem, but it also is the name given to the first beat, the beginning of the groove or moment of impact associated with James Brown, Mr Dynamite himself. When I feel that I am in the therapeutic groove, I know I am doing all I can to help the volunteer. There is a natural flow to our conversation. I am more likely to be in the groove when I am focused exclusively on the volunteer and forget about the existence of the audience.

I am aware that the concept of 'helping the person' is very vague, but in my conversations, I seek to work with the level of specificity of goal that is most meaningful to the volunteer. This means that while I am informed by the acronym 'SMART'[2] when it comes to goal setting, I do not use it exclusively in my work. I will discuss helping volunteers to set goals later in the chapter.

Demonstrating therapy in action

My next goal is one that is more audience-focused than volunteer-focused: it is to demonstrate the approach to therapy that the audience expects to see. As I said in Chapter 1, at the events where I demonstrate therapy live, people are expecting to see me practise either REBT or CBT or see me practise in my own way free from any label. This context guides me, but not if it means withholding a potentially helpful intervention with a volunteer. Let me say a little more about this.

Demonstrating REBT

When the audience expects a demonstration of REBT, then I will endeavour to show the following skills. I will help the volunteer to identify a target problem and provide an example of this problem, which I will assess using the ABC framework of REBT outlined in the left-hand column of Table 3.1. In particular, I will encourage the person to assume temporarily that the adversity that we have identified at 'A' is true. I do this to help them to identify the rigid and extreme attitudes at 'B' that underpin their problematic response at 'C' and their alternative flexible and non-extreme attitudes that account for their healthy response to the assumed-to-be-true adversity at 'A'. Then, I will help the person to stand back and examine and question these two sets of attitudes and to commit themself to developing the latter set rather than the former. In doing this, I will try my best to engage the volunteer emotionally as we work together to discover ways of implementing their flexible and/or non-extreme beliefs in the face of the adversity at 'A'. I hope to conclude the conversation with the person resolving to put what they learn into practice as soon as possible. Particularly towards the end of the conversation, I will be looking to help the volunteer to generalise their learning.

I practise REBT quite broadly, but when I demonstrate it in the context I am discussing in this book, I aim to show its classic aspects as would Ellis in his demonstrations (see Dryden & Ellis, 2003).

Demonstrating CBT

When I am expected to demonstrate CBT, I still may keep to the above framework as CBT is a tradition not defined by any single approach and REBT is a specific approach within this tradition. However, I may be more generic in my interventions than when I demonstrate REBT. Thus, I may help the volunteer to examine distorted inferences at 'A' instead of encouraging them to assume that these inferences are true as a way of identifying their underlying rigid and extreme attitudes as I would in REBT. Also, I may encourage the volunteer to accept mindfully the presence of certain troublesome cognitions rather than to change them as I would in REBT. Or I might encourage them to accept, again mindfully, their problematic emotions rather than to target these emotions for change, again as I would in REBT. CBT is a broad umbrella, and thus I can use all of its spokes when demonstrating it. However, as noted at the beginning of this section, my CBT demonstrations are largely informed by REBT.

Doing my own thing: 'Windy Dryden in action'

The VBTCs that I enjoy the most, if I am honest, are those where I am given free rein to intervene as I, Windy Dryden, see fit, without the constraints of having to demonstrate REBT or CBT because this is what the audience expects due to the advertising of the event. Now, some members of the audience may still expect to see me practise REBT in this 'Windy Dryden in action' type of event, as I am most closely associated me with this approach. However, as the event has not been advertised as a 'Windy Dryden demonstrates REBT' event, I am committed to having conversations as I see fit.

In this 'doing my own thing', 'Windy Dryden in action' event, I may still largely practise REBT or CBT, but I will do so in my own way.[3] Indeed, I may have a very different conversation if the situation requires it. The conversation that I had with 'Carla' (in Chapter 12) is a good example of this and draws as much upon the 'transformational chairwork' approach of Kellogg (2015) as it does upon REBT/CBT. I have referred to the way I practise in general as 'flexibility-based CBT' (Dryden, 2018). This approach is underpinned by the principles of REBT and CBT, but is also pluralistic in the stance that I take since I draw from a range of other approaches to help clients and, in the present context, volunteers reach their goals.

Educating the audience

My final purpose is to educate the audience. In doing so, I offer them a perspective of how to understand a variety of common emotional and behavioural problems. I also offer them a model of how to help their clients (if they are professionals) and themselves (if they both professionals and non-professionals) in dealing with these problems.

Helping the volunteer to set realistic goals

The second area where goals are important in VBTCs concerns what the volunteer wants to gain from the conversation. My approach to such conversations is to take a problem-focused, solution-orientated approach. In practice, this means that, most often, I will set goals with the volunteer once when we have both assessed their problem.[4] If I ask for goals before problem assessment, then I may encounter some goal-related difficulties as discussed below.

Dealing with problematic goals

The following are goals that volunteers express that are problematic and how I tend to respond when I encounter them in VBTCs.

The volunteer's goal is vague

The volunteer may set a vague goal, and if so, it is important that I help them to make this goal as specific as possible. Examples of vague goals are: 'I want to be content with my life', 'I want to get over my guilt' and 'I want to get on with my life'. Here, I may use the 'SMART' acronym that I mentioned earlier (see Note 2).

The volunteer wants to change 'A'

Sometimes the volunteer may wish to change the 'A' (in the ABC framework – see Table 3.1), either the actual situation and/or the adversity, rather than change their unconstructive responses to the 'A' to those that are constructive. If this is the case and 'A' can be changed, I help them to understand that the best chance they have to change 'A' is when they are in a healthy frame of mind to do so. They can achieve this by making their responses to this 'A' constructive. So before they can change 'A', they need to change their disturbed responses at 'C'.

When the volunteer wants to change another person

When the volunteer has a problem involving their relationship with another person, for example, then their goal may be to change that person. I respond by helping them to see that this goal is inappropriate as another's behaviour is not under the direct control of the volunteer. By contrast, attempts to influence the other person are under the volunteer's direct control and *may* lead to such behavioural change. As such, the goal of attempting to influence the other person is an appropriate goal. If I have time, I also help the volunteer consider their responses if their influence attempts do not work. Helping a volunteer to deal constructively with such failed attempts is often important.

The best time for a volunteer to influence another person for the better is when they are in a healthy, not a disturbed frame of mind. Thus, if the volunteer is in a disturbed frame of mind and wishes to change another person, I am faced with two tasks. First, I need to provide them with an acceptable rationale for negotiating an 'addressing disturbance' goal. I then need to help them understand that it is important to set a goal that is within their control (i.e. their behaviour) rather than the outcome of their behaviour (which is outside their control).

When the volunteer sets a goal based on experiencing less of the problematic response

Often when asked to state their goal about the adversity at 'A', a volunteer may say that they want to feel less of the disturbed emotion that features in their target problem (e.g. less anxious). REBT theory, which largely underpins my approach to goal negotiation, argues that when a volunteer holds a rigid attitude, they take a preference (e.g. for acceptance) and transform it into a rigid attitude (e.g. 'I want to be accepted, and therefore I have to be'). When they hold a flexible attitude, they take the same preference and keep it flexible by negating possible rigidity (e.g. 'I want to be accepted, but it is not necessary that I am'). In both the rigid attitude and the flexible attitude, the strength of the unhealthy negative emotion in the first case and of the healthy negative emotion in the second is determined by the strength of the preference when that preference has not been met. The stronger the preference under these circumstances, the stronger the negative emotion of both types. Based on this analysis, my goal is to help the volunteer experience a healthy negative emotion of relative intensity to the unhealthy negative emotion rather than to encourage them to strive to experience an unhealthy negative emotion of decreased intensity.

When a volunteer sets a goal based on experiencing the absence of their problematic response

I am also prepared when the volunteer nominates the absence of the problem as their goal (e.g. 'I don't want to feel anxious when giving a talk'). When the volunteer says this, I help them to see that it is not possible to live in a response vacuum and from there I can discuss the presence of a set of healthy responses to their adversity as their goal.

When a volunteer sets as a goal a positive response to the actual situation and bypasses the adversity

Another scenario may occur when I ask a volunteer for their goal is that they may nominate a positive response to the actual situation while bypassing the adversity. For example, let's suppose that a volunteer is anxious about their mind going blank when giving a public talk. If they say that their goal is to become confident at giving public presentations, they would have bypassed dealing with the adversity of their mind going blank. In this case, I would ask the volunteer how they can become confident at giving public presentations as long as they are anxious about their mind going blank. By helping this volunteer to deal with this issue first and to set an appropriate goal concerning their adversity, I would be making it possible for them later to develop the increased confidence that they are seeking.

When a volunteer wants to feel indifferent in the face of an adversity

Sometimes a volunteer says that their goal is not to care about a particular adversity when, in reality, they do care about it. Indeed, their disturbed feelings indicate that they care. My practice is to help the person understand what not caring or indifference means as follows:

WINDY: Now Mickleover Sports are playing Rushall Olympic on Saturday in the Evo-Stich Premier Division. Do you care who wins?

VOLUNTEER: Not at all.

WINDY: That is what not caring means. Faced with a choice between two options you can't choose between them because you don't care what happens. Now when you say you want not to care if your mind goes blank when you speak in public, do you mean that faced with the choice of your mind going blank or it not going blank you want me to help you to be indifferent about the outcome?

VOLUNTEER: I guess not.

WINDY: Because would you prefer your mind to go blank or not to go blank?

VOLUNTEER: Not to go blank.

WINDY: So rather than not caring if your mind goes blank, how about if I help you to care about it, but not to be disturbed about it should it happen?

VOLUNTEER: Yes, that makes sense.

I would then help the volunteer understand what the behavioural and cognitive referents of non-disturbed caring would be so that they could strive for this psychological state.

What constitutes 'good' goals in VBTCs

If the above goals are problematic, what constitutes 'good' goals in VBTCs? The following goals are those with which I prefer to work in my demonstrations and that I strive to help volunteers to set.

Goals with respect to the person's disturbed response to the adversity

It is a hallmark of the conversations that I have with volunteers that I strive to help them to identify the adversity that features in their problem and then to help them set realistic goals for responding to the adversity when they are disturbed about it. I noted above people's tendency to bypass adversities when dealing with their problems and while this may help them in the short term, unfortunately, it tends not to work in the longer term. So although the conversation that I have with a volunteer is very brief, my ideal aim is to help them deal effectively with the problem-related adversity when they are disturbed about it.

According to the ABC framework that often guides my assessment of a volunteer's target problem[5] (see Table 3.1), the experiential aspects of the person's problem (i.e. how they feel, the thoughts that accompany these feelings and their actions) occur at 'C'. These are in response to the rigid and extreme attitudes that they hold at 'B' about the adversity at 'A'. When the person experiences the problem, these 'C' responses tend to comprise an unhealthy negative emotion, highly distorted and ruminative thinking and unconstructive behaviour.[6] If I am successful in my interventions at this point, I will help the volunteer to set a goal where they will experience a healthy negative emotion, balanced and non-ruminative thinking and constructive behaviour.

The volunteer may well struggle with setting a healthy negative emotion as an emotional goal in the face of the adversity. I explain the value of doing so as follows:

- An adversity is a negative event for the volunteer.
- Given this, it is not realistic for them to have a positive emotion about it.
- Neither is it realistic for them to have a neutral reaction to it.
- Therefore, they will have a negative emotional response to it.
- Their choice is to have a negative emotion that is healthy or one that is unhealthy.
- A healthy negative emotion has a negative-feeling tone, but is healthy in that it helps the person to face the adversity, to process it and to change it if it can be changed or to adjust constructively to it if it can't be changed.
- An unhealthy negative emotion also has a negative-feeling tone but is unhealthy in that it interferes with the person facing the adversity and processing it and thus makes it much harder for them to change it if it can be changed or to adjust constructively to it if it can't be changed.

In general, the time that it takes me to help the person construct a healthy but realistic way of responding to the adversity is time well spent.

Goals with respect to changing the adversity when the person is not disturbed about it

In ongoing therapy, once I have helped the person deal with their disturbed response to the adversity, I help them to set goals with respect to changing the adversity (if it can be changed). Ordinarily, in VBTCs, I don't have time to do both, so I agree with the volunteer that we will concentrate on the former situation. However, sometimes it is clear that the volunteer does not have a disturbed response to the adversity, but has not been successful at changing it when it can be changed and wants to do so. Under these circumstances, I explain that I can only set a goal with the person that is within, what Covey (1989) calls, their 'sphere of influence' rather than their 'sphere of concern'. The former covers what the person is in control of (e.g. their behaviour), while the latter covers what the person is concerned with, but not directly in control of (i.e. the outcomes of their behaviour).

In setting 'sphere of influence' goals, I first review with the volunteer what influence attempts they have already made and what the outcomes of these attempts were so that I only devote the limited time we have to discussing what they have not tried and what its likely outcome might be. Once we have selected a 'sphere of influence' goal, then I help the person to identify any obstacles to implementing it and set goals with respect to these obstacles. This may seem a lot to accomplish in 30 minutes, but it is surprising what can be accomplished when a focus is created and maintained. This brings me to the more technical parts of the way I conduct VBTCs.

Notes

1 Examples of such topics are 'dealing with anxiety', 'dealing with rejection', 'envy and jealousy', 'dealing with problematic anger', 'dating without disturbance' and 'overcoming procrastination', amongst others.
2 'SMART' goals are those that are specific ('S'), measurable ('M'), achievable ('A'), relevant and realistic ('R') and time-bound ('T').
3 Because I can't make clear to the audience what I am doing at the same time as being deeply involved in a conversation with a volunteer, I spend time, once the conversation has finished, answering questions from the audience concerning why I intervened in the way that I did and how this was based on REBT/CBT.
4 Sometimes, I take a solution-orientated stance at the outset without first focusing on the volunteer's problem. This is where the event at which I am demonstrating how I work has a coaching or development focus.
5 The problem that the volunteer and I agree to focus on is known as the 'target problem'.
6 Such unconstructive behaviour may take the form of overt actions or action tendencies that the person does not act on.

Chapter 5

Task behaviour in VBTCs

In the working alliance framework, the task component of the alliance in VBTCs concerns what I do as a therapist and what the volunteer does to help the latter achieve their goal. In this chapter, I will concentrate on explicating my task in guiding the conversation in a goal-directed way. But first, let me outline what I believe the volunteer's tasks are in the process, for without the volunteer's participation, what I do counts for very little.

The volunteer's tasks in a VBTC

If you recall, when I call for a volunteer to take part in a very brief and hopefully therapeutic conversation in front of the attendant audience, I stress that the person should ideally be prepared to discuss a genuine problem and one for which they are seeking help. When a person volunteers to participate in a VBTC, they are engaging in important volunteer task behaviour when they state what the problem is and actively engage with me in clarifying the problem and what they want to gain from our conversation. It is important that they answer my questions as honestly as possible and are prepared to select and discuss a specific example of the problem. In short, they need to be able to think carefully and quickly about a range of issues.

Another important volunteer task is to give me feedback on any hypothesis I might make about the factors that account for their problem. Their active agreement is important here as we need to target these factors for discussion and possible change. I would rather the person explicitly disagree with my hypothesis than be compliant on the surface but privately disagree with me. While I am speaking with a volunteer, I will look out for possible compliance and will ask the person to put into their own words what they hear me saying and also to give me their honest response to my points. At this juncture, I stress that I am happy to make any modification to my hypothesis based on their feedback.

Linked to the above, it is important that the volunteer shares with me any doubts, reservations and objections (DROs) to any aspect of our conversation and not just to any hypothesis I might make at the assessment phase of the session.

Along similar lines, it is important that the volunteer actively engages with me when I invite them to stand back and question the attitudes that we have both identified as underpinning their problem. Following on from this, it is also central that the person works with me to formulate healthy alternatives to these attitudes that will help them to achieve their goal.

Stating what they are prepared to do to achieve their goal as a result of our attitude-focused discussion is a central volunteer task, as is putting this into practice after we have concluded our conversation.

My tasks in VBTCs

Now that I have outlined the volunteer's tasks in a VBTC, let me concentrate on my task-related behaviour.

Empowering the volunteer

Before I outline some of the specific tasks that I have in VBTCs, I want to make the point that overall I see my role as helping the person to get the most out of the very brief time that we have together. There are a number of ways in which I do this and I will do so when the moment presents itself. Thus, I will discover and encourage the volunteer to use one or more of the following in the service of personal problem-solving:

- *The internal strengths that the person has.* Persistence and open-mindedness are particularly valuable strengths in VBTCs.
- *The external resources to which the person can gain access and use.* Identifying others who can support the person in the change process after the end of the conversation can be particularly helpful.
- *The values that the person may have that might serve as motivators for change.* Later on in this chapter, I discuss how I use the concept of cognitive dissonance in VBTCs. Knowing the person's key values helps me to do this.

- *The role models they have that may serve to inspire them during the process.* A role model that demonstrates the quality of struggling in the face of adversity, but triumphing in the end, is particularly helpful.
- *Positive experiences of being helped that might be reproduced during the VBTC.* This is particularly relevant for me in that it gives me ideas for how to best help the person.
- *How they have helped themselves in the past.* If relevant, they may be able to reproduce this process in addressing their target problem.
- *Any instances of experiencing change in a short period of time, elements of which might be used in the VBTC.* Sometimes people have changed quite quickly, and if so, there may be lessons to be learned from that experience that can be applied to a VBTC.
- *Their preferred learning style.* This can help me in any suggestions that I might make concerning how the person can address their problem.
- *Help-related maxims that may be used at various points during the process.* An example might be 'Do or do not. There is no try'. This was a favourite maxim of one of my volunteers. When he said, "I'll try to do 'x'," I reminded him of it, which helped him to make a definite commitment to do 'x'.

Creating and maintaining a problem focus

Having invited members of the audience to come up to discuss a problem with me, I tend to begin the conversation with a volunteer like this: "What problem would you like some help with today?" Having created the problem focus, I will then keep to it and help the person to express the problem from their perspective. My task at this point is to understand it from the person's perspective and then to assess it. A volunteer may bring up a number of problems with which they would like help, but as I only have time to help them to deal with one problem in the time at my disposal, I invite them to select one. I refer to the volunteer's selected problem as the 'target problem'.

While selecting a target problem may be quite straightforward, at other times I have found that it is important to spend time with the volunteer in order to fully understand what the problem is, as it may not be quite what it appears at first glance. This is particularly the case with problems of 'anger'. While it is sometimes true that a volunteer's problem with anger involves just anger, sometimes the anger masks a more important problem with anxiety, shame or hurt. Spending some time at the outset exploring the complexity of a volunteer's problem is time usefully spent and helps the person set goals in line with the true nature of their problem.

Problem and meta-problem

When a person nominates a problem with which they would like help, they may have what is called a 'meta-problem' – literally a problem about their nominated problem. Consider Samantha who volunteered for a VBTC in New York in 2008. Initially, Samantha wanted to discuss her unhealthy anger-related problem when dealing with frustration, but she also felt ashamed of the way she reacted when she experienced anger. During the conversation, she 'shuttled' back and forth from the problem to the meta-problem even though she stated that the existence of the meta-problem would not affect the work that we needed to do on the primary problem.[1] In this case, I had to be quite firm with Samantha and refused to discuss the meta-problem of shame until we had concluded our work on the primary problem of unhealthy anger.

I use three criteria in working with a meta-problem before the primary problem. The first criterion is when the existence of the meta-problem interferes or is likely to interfere with our conversation about the primary problem in the demonstration session. The second criterion is when the existence of the meta-problem is likely to interfere outside the session with the work that the volunteer needs to do to address their primary problem effectively. The final criterion is that the volunteer can see the sense of making the meta-problem their target problem. I make the first two explicit to the volunteer, but will go along with the volunteer if they want to keep the focus on the primary problem even though the meta-problem may interfere, in which case, as with Samantha, I will be quite firm with the volunteer in keeping the agreed focus on the primary, target problem.

Seeking the volunteer's permission to interrupt

I mentioned in Chapter 2 the importance of seeking a volunteer's permission to interrupt them. This is particularly the case if I am going to maintain a problem focus once I have created one. Some volunteers will wander from problem to problem or away from the problem altogether, and if I allow this, then we will not get anywhere with our conversation. So, when needed, I will interrupt the volunteer to maintain a focus on their target problem and will do so with tact and, if appropriate, humour once I have their permission to do so.

Working with a specific example of the target problem

Having agreed to work with the volunteer's target problem, it is useful, whenever possible, to work with a specific example of that problem. The purpose of working with such an example is that it helps the volunteer to identify their specific responses, and these help me to identify what they were most disturbed about in the situation (i.e. the adversity). A specific example follows the rules of the game of 'Cluedo',[2] where one has to identify a specific person who committed a specific murder in a specific place with a specific murder weapon.

A specific example of the target problem might be one that:

- Happened recently.
- Is typical.
- Is vivid or memorable.
- Is anticipated.

My preference is to work with an anticipated example of the target problem as long as this is likely to be imminent. The reason for this is that working with such a future example helps the person to think how they might handle an adversity differently without actually having had a problematic response to the adversity. In dealing with a past specific example of the volunteer's problem, they still have to apply any learning to a future example, so I have found it best to assess the anticipated example even though it hasn't yet happened. Having said this, if it is unlikely that the person will encounter the adversity imminently, then dealing a past specific example of their problem may yield richer data.

Keeping the focus on the specific example

Once the volunteer and I have decided to focus on a specific example of their target problem, then it is my job to keep them focused on that example so that I can help them to assess it properly. I need to do this because, while having a conversation, many people have a natural tendency to move from the specific to the general. Again, I have found that asking them for permission to interrupt them and refocus the conversation on the specific example is an important skill. Other effective ways of helping keep the focus on the specific example that I use are encouraging the person to visualise the setting in which the example happened and asking the person to describe what happened as though it were occurring in the present, using the present tense as they do so.

Assessing the problem

In my experience, arriving at a shared and accurate assessment of the problem, usually through the chosen specific example, is possibly the key to the volunteer deriving some benefit from the conversation. I mentioned in Chapter 1 that there is no available time to carry out a case conceptualization in this helping context, so problem assessment is particularly important.

Using the Situational ABC framework

When I use the 'Situational ABC' framework (see Table 3.1) to assess the specific example of the person's target problem, I will assess the 'situation', 'A' and 'C' in whatever order the person tends to speak about them. However, I tend only to assess 'B' when I have understood the other three variables. Having clarified this, in this book, I will discuss 'C', the 'situation' and 'A' in that order.

'C'

When the person experiences their problem, often it is because they feel disturbed emotions, have distressing thoughts and/or images and act (or feel like acting) in a way that is unconstructive for them from a longer-term perspective, even though doing so may bring them short-term relief or even satisfaction.

In my conversation with the volunteer, it is very important for me to discover and work with the person's main unhealthy negative emotion. This is to ensure that the conversation has an affective quality that engages the volunteer's interest and that of the audience, but doing so gives me clues about the possible theme of the adversity at 'A' (see Table 5.1).

At times, it may only become clear if the person's emotion at 'C' is disturbed by inspecting the overt behaviour or action tendencies that accompany the emotion. For example, if a person's anger is unhealthy,

Table 5.1 Unhealthy negative emotions and the adversities to which they point

Unhealthy Negative Emotion	Adversity
• Anxiety	• Threat
• Depression	• Loss; failure; undeserved plight
• Guilt	• Breaking or failing to live up to one's moral code; hurting someone's feelings
• Shame	• Falling very short of an ideal; negative evaluation of self by others
• Hurt	• Someone significant to the volunteer is not as invested in the relationship as the volunteer is
• Unhealthy anger	• Someone transgresses the volunteer's personal domain; another poses a threat to the volunteer's self-esteem; another 'shames' or ridicules the person
• Unhealthy jealousy	• A threat is posed to the volunteer's relationship by someone deemed to be a rival
• Unhealthy envy	• Someone has something that the volunteer desires, but does not have

it tends to be accompanied by attack and confrontation, while if it is healthy, it tends to be characterised by assertion and conciliation. Appendix 1 lists the major unhealthy negative emotions that volunteers frequently bring as problems and their behavioural referents (overt actions and action tendencies). I use such information to help myself and the volunteer to decide whether or not their emotional 'C' is disturbed where there is doubt when focusing on their emotions alone.

The 'situation'

The situation is a descriptive account of the specific context in which the volunteer experienced their problem. It represents what Maultsby (1984) has called the 'camera check'. By this, he meant that a situation is what a camera with an audio-channel records; nothing more, nothing less. Thus, the situation is devoid of inferences that tend to feature in 'A' (see below).

'A'

'A' stands for an 'adversity', which is a negative event that either occurred in the situation discussed above or was deemed to occur in the situation. 'A's are frequently inferences about the situation towards which the person has a problematic response. An 'inference' is an interpretation that goes beyond the data at hand and may be correct or incorrect. In my experience, 'A' is what the person is most disturbed about and represents the adversity that often forms the focus of my therapeutic conversation with the volunteer. As I have noted, my preference in VBTCs, whenever I can, is to help the volunteer deal effectively with their problem-related adversity. To do that, I need to assess it carefully. How I do this may vary, but I use the person's disturbed emotion to drive my questioning, and I also state what the situation is.

In demonstrating how I assess 'A', I will discuss a typical problem that a volunteer may present. Let's imagine that Don has volunteered for help with a problem. He is anxious about going on a first date with a woman. His major disturbed emotion at 'C' is anxiety, and the 'situation' is a first date. Here are a few examples of questions that I might ask to identify 'A':

- When you think about going on a first date and you feel anxious about it, what are you most anxious about?
- What is most anxiety-creating in your mind about going on a first date?
- When you are anxious about going on a first date, what is your anxiety most closely connected to (or related to)?

Sometimes a volunteer may respond with a highly distorted inference at 'C' rather than the adversity at 'A', in which case I need to explain why this happens[3] and refocus them on identifying 'A'. For this reason, I developed a technique to identify 'A' called 'Windy's Magic Question' (see Box 5.1).

Box 5.1 Windy's Magic Question

The purpose of this questioning technique is to help the volunteer to identify the 'A' in the Situational ABC framework as quickly as possible (i.e. what the client is most disturbed about) once 'C' has been assessed and the 'situation' in which 'C' has occurred has been identified and briefly described.

Step 1: I ask the volunteer to focus on their disturbed emotional 'C' (here, 'anxiety').

Step 2: I have the person focus on the situation in which 'C' occurred (here, 'going on a first date').

Step 3: I ask the person: "Which ingredient could we give you to eliminate or significantly reduce 'C' (here, anxiety)?" (in this case, the person "not being boring"). I take care that the person does not change the situation (i.e. he does not say: "not going on the date").

Step 4: The opposite is probably 'A' (e.g. "being boring"), but I check to see if this is the case. I ask: "So when you are on a first date are you most anxious about being boring?" If not, I use the question again until the person confirms what they are most anxious about in the described situation.

Encouraging the volunteer to assume temporarily that 'A' is true

Once I have helped the volunteer to identify 'A', I encourage them to assume temporarily that it is true. I do this because this is the best way of helping the person to identify the rigid and extreme attitudes that underpin their disturbed responses to the adversity at 'C'. There may be an opportunity later to help the person question 'A' if it appears distorted.

Helping the volunteer set an adversity-related goal

Once I have helped the person to identify their disturbed responses to the adversity at 'A' and the nature of the adversity, I then ask them what their goal is in handling the adversity. This sometimes comes as a shock to them because they want to handle the situation better rather than deal with the adversity. Let me show you what I mean in the following exchange between Don and myself[4]:

WINDY: So, to sum up, with respect to going on a first date, you are anxious about the prospect of 'being boring'. Is that right?

DON: Yes, that's correct.

WINDY: How would you like to handle 'being boring'?

DON: Oh! I don't want to be boring.

WINDY: I understand that, but is it a possibility?

DON: Yes, I guess it is. I'm sorry to say.

WINDY: And does being anxious about 'being boring' help you on first dates or not?

DON: Definitely not.

WINDY: So since 'being boring' is a possibility on a first date and being anxious about it doesn't help, should we aim for a feeling response to 'being boring' that is more constructive?

DON: That would be a great idea.

WINDY: What would you call that response?

DON: I'm not sure. Being less anxious?

[This is a typical response to a question that seeks a healthy negative emotion. I discussed the problem with 'less disturbed' goals in Chapter 4 in the section entitled, 'When the volunteer sets a goal based on experiencing less of the problematic response'. In this case, what I will do is to help construct a case for the healthy negative emotion and ask the volunteer to suggest a name for it. If they still struggle, I will suggest a name. Notice below how I offer my view to Don and ask his permission to state it.]

WINDY: Would you like to hear my view on this issue?

DON: Yes, please.

WINDY: OK. So we need a response that (a) acknowledges that you 'being boring' on a first date is a possibility, (b) recognises that it is not something you want to happen, but (c) is free from anxiety. Is that right?

DON: Yes.

WINDY: What would you call the emotion that has these features?

DON: Concerned?

WINDY: Exactly. How would you like to be able to handle 'being boring' by being concerned, but not anxious about it?

[I often suggest a healthy negative emotion by negating the unhealthy negative emotion alternative. In this case, 'concerned, but not anxious'.]

DON: That would be great.

Asking for an open-ended goal

Sometimes, I may ask the volunteer more broadly what their goal is at this point. While I do not think this is good practice – because the focus is taken off the adversity – I have included it here to show you that it is possible to rescue a situation even in a VBTC. Thus, in what follows, I ask Don more broadly what his goal is without mentioning the adversity.

WINDY: So, to sum up, with respect to going on a first date, you are anxious about the prospect of being boring. Is that right?
DON: Yes, that's correct.
WINDY: What would you like to achieve from our conversation today?

[My goal question is broad and it is the type of question that I might ask at the very beginning of a conversation with a volunteer. Let's see what happens when I ask it at this point.]

DON: I would like to feel more confident about going on first dates.

[Note that Don has bypassed the adversity of 'being boring' and gone to set a goal in relation to the situation and not in relation to the adversity. However, all is not lost, and look how I connect the two goals in the following exchanges.]

WINDY: I see. What would best help you to develop that confidence, being anxious about 'being boring', concerned, but not anxious about 'being boring' or unconcerned about 'being boring'?

[My question includes the 'indifference' option because some people seek that as their goal with respect to adversity and if Don nominates it as his goal, then I will need to discuss the implausibility of this option.]

DON: How can I be unconcerned?
WINDY: By lying to yourself and saying that it does not matter if you are boring or interesting when it does! So it's not a realistic option. But what will help you develop confidence on first dates being anxious about 'being boring' or concerned, but not anxious about it?
DON: Concerned, but not anxious about it.
WINDY: Would you like me to help you do that?
DON: Yes, please.

[What I have done is to help Don see that the route to dating confidence is through becoming concerned, but not anxious about 'being boring' and that this will become the goal of our conversation.]

'B'

I have now assessed the following components: 'the situation', 'A', 'C' and the client's adversity-related goal. According to the 'Situational ABC' model that I use in conducting VBTCs, the main reason the volunteer has a problem about the adversity question is that they hold a rigid and extreme attitude towards this adversity. My main task at this point is to help the volunteer to understand that 'A' does not determine 'C', but rather 'B' largely determines 'C'. There are many ways to do this, but the most efficient is one that I developed called 'Windy's Review Assessment Procedure' (WRAP). Box 5.2 shows how to use this technique with Don, who we met earlier in this chapter.

Box 5.2 Windy's Review Assessment Procedure (WRAP)

Purpose: Once 'C' (e.g. 'anxiety') and 'A' (e.g. 'my mind going blank') have been assessed, this technique can be used to identify both the volunteer's rigid and alterative flexible attitudes and to help the person to understand the two relevant B–C connections. This technique can also be used with any of the derivatives of the rigid and flexible attitude pairing.

Step 1: I say: "Let's review what we know and what we don't know so far."

Step 2: I then say: "We know four things. First, we know that you are anxious ('C'). Second, we know that you are anxious about being boring ('A'). Third, we know that your goal with respect to the problem is to feel concerned, but not anxious about being boring and – this is an educated guess on my part – we know that it is important to you that you are not boring on a first date. Am I correct?"

Assuming that the volunteer confirms your hunch, note that what I have done is to identify the part of the attitude that is common to both the volunteer's rigid attitude and alternative flexible attitude, as we will see.

Step 3: Now, I say: "Now let's review what we don't know. This is where I need your help. We don't know which of two attitudes your anxiety is based on. So, when you are anxious about being boring on a first date, is your anxiety based on Attitude 1: 'It is important to me that I am not boring on a first date and therefore I must not be boring' ('rigid attitude') or Attitude 2: 'It is important to me that I am not boring on a first date, but that does not mean that I must not be boring' ('flexible attitude')?"

Step 4: If necessary, I help the volunteer to understand that their anxiety is based on their rigid attitude if they are unsure.

Step 5: Once the volunteer is clear that their anxiety is based on their rigid attitude, I make and emphasise the rigid attitude–disturbed 'C' connection. Then I ask: "Now let's suppose instead that you had a strong conviction in Attitude 2; how would you feel about being boring on a first date if you strongly believed that while it was important to you that you are not boring on first date, it did not follow that you must not be boring?"

Step 6: If necessary, I help the volunteer to understand that this attitude will help them to achieve their goal of feeling concerned, but not anxious about the adversity. As I do so, emphasise the flexible attitude–healthy 'C' connection.

Step 7: I then ensure that the volunteer clearly understands the differences between the two B–C connections.

Step 8: Next, I help the volunteer to recommit to unanxious concern as their emotional goal in this situation and encourage them to see that developing conviction in their flexible attitude is the best way of achieving this goal.

In using the WRAP method, I achieve the following. I help the volunteer:

* Understand the *general* point that attitudes about an adversity largely determine a person's responses to this adversity.

- Understand the specific points that: (i) a rigid attitude largely determines a disturbed response to the adversity; and (ii) a flexible attitude largely determines a healthy response to the same adversity.
- See that changing their attitude from rigid to flexible will help them to achieve their adversity-related goal.

It is important to note that while I have discussed the use of the 'WRAP' technique when helping the volunteer differentiate between their rigid attitude and their flexible attitude, it can also be used to help the person differentiate between any of their extreme attitudes and their non-extreme attitudes.[5]

Addressing the problem

Once the volunteer and I have agreed on the assessment of their problem and what a possible solution might look like, I then shift the conversation to a discussion of how the person may address the problem.

In modern CBT, there seem to be two different groups of therapeutic strategies: change-based strategies and acceptance-based strategies

Change-based strategies

As the name makes explicit, change-based strategies are employed to help people change problematic psychological processes, and I use such strategies freely in VBTCs. After I have carried out the problem assessment, my main task is to help the volunteer to stand back and examine their rigid and flexible attitudes and/or their extreme and non-extreme attitudes.

Examining and changing attitudes. When I encourage the volunteer to examine their rigid and flexible attitudes, for example, I have the goal of helping them to change their rigid attitude to its flexible alternative.[6] However, I do try to be fair-minded in the process. There is a formal structure that I can use when encouraging a volunteer to examine their rigid–flexible attitude pairing (Dryden, 2015). Thus, I can ask the person which of the rigid–flexible attitude pairings is true and which is false, which is logical and which is illogical and which is helpful and which unhelpful. I often use this structure, but in doing so I am looking for persuasive ways of encouraging attitude change.

The issue of what is a persuasive argument for a volunteer is an interesting one, and I am not sure that I have any particular insight to offer here. However, let me outline a few of the factors that I take into account when striving to increase the persuasiveness of my attitude change strategies.

'Teach your children well'. When I use this technique, I take the rigid–flexible attitude pairing and ask the volunteer which of the two attitudes they would teach a child and explain the reason for their choice. Then, I invite them to commit themself to developing this attitude for themself and to have them deal with any obstacle to doing so.

Experiences of attitude change. It can be helpful to discover the volunteer's experiences of changing their attitudes and what were the processes involved in bringing about such changes. I then seek to use these processes to help the person to change their rigid attitude to a flexible attitude and/or their extreme attitude to its non-extreme alternative.

Ask the volunteer for persuasive arguments. George Kelly, the originator of the psychology of personal constructs, has often been quoted as saying that if you want to know anything about the client, ask them – they may tell you (Bannister & Fransella, 1986). With this in mind, I sometimes ask the volunteer what arguments they would find persuasive in changing their rigid/extreme attitude to a flexible/ non-extreme attitude, and occasionally they have told me.

Humour. In Chapter 2, I discussed my use of humour in VBTCs. Sometimes it was something I said that the volunteer found funny that was the turning point for them in the attitude change process. When this occurs, I think what happens on these occasions is that what I said helps the person to stand back, see the ridiculousness of their rigid or extreme attitude and resolve to change their point of view.

Inducing and helping the person to resolve a state of cognitive dissonance. A state of cognitive dissonance exists when the volunteer realises that they hold two attitudes that are inconsistent with one another and that something must change to eliminate the dissonance. For example, I often portray a rigid attitude as one that is fundamentalist by nature. I then ask the volunteer if they are democratic or authoritarian in basic outlook. Once they have said that they hold a democratic outlook, I ask them whether the rigid attitude on which we are focusing is an example of a democratic outlook or an authoritarian outlook. They reluctantly admit that it is an example of the authoritarian outlook and, in doing so, they become aware of their state of dissonance. They are now open to the possibility of change. I then say that they can resolve their dissonance in three ways. First, they can change their basic democratic outlook to an authoritarian one. Second, they can change their rigid attitude to a flexible one. And third, they can accept the state of dissonance. This latter option is quite difficult as cognitive dissonance theory notes that humans have a strong drive to eliminate states of dissonance. I then ask them which route they wish to take. Invariably, they say the second route, and I use this to encourage them to develop the flexible version of their attitude so that this is consistent with their overall democratic outlook.

Helping the volunteer to move from intellectual insight to emotional insight. It is clear that in the course of a conversation lasting 30 minutes or less, it is very unlikely that the person will achieve the type of attitude change that will make a significant difference to how they feel or the way they act. However, sometimes they do have an epiphany that will help them on the path towards such change. This raises the question concerning what the process of attitude change is. To help us understand this, Ellis (1963) distinguished between 'intellectual' insight and 'emotional' insight. When a volunteer has intellectual insight, they understand that their rigid attitude, for example, is false, illogical and unhelpful and that the alternative flexible attitude is true, logical and helpful, but they have little conviction in these points. They may say such things as, "I understand it in my head, but not in my heart." Intellectual insight has little impact on the person's emotions and behaviour. By contrast, when a volunteer has emotional insight, they have a lot of conviction in the above points and say such things as, "I really understand this not only in my head, but also in my heart." Emotional insight does impact on the person's emotions and behaviour. Here are a few things that I do to encourage the volunteer to move towards emotional insight and thus change their attitude.

Intrapersonal and interpersonal dialogues. In an intrapersonal dialogue, I promote a conversation between two different parts of the volunteer; for example, with one representing the rigid or extreme attitude and the other representing the flexible or non-extreme attitude. While the purpose of this dialogue is to encourage conviction in the latter, what the person sometimes expresses is an obstacle to this process, which I can then address with the volunteer. An example of an intrapersonal dialogue occurs in Chapter 12.

In an interpersonal dialogue, I promote a conversation between the volunteer and a person (living or dead) in the volunteer's life with whom they have 'unfinished business'. Wherever possible, I encourage the volunteer to speak to the other person while holding the flexible or non-extreme versions of their attitude. If possible, I strive to encourage the person to finish the 'unfinished business'.

Imagery rehearsal. When I use imagery rehearsal in a VBTC, I do so in one of two ways. First, I encourage the person to imagine disturbing themself by holding a rigid attitude about a relevant adversity and then responding to that adversity by changing their rigid attitude to a flexible one. I then help them to see that they can use this technique to prepare to address the adversity or at any other time. Second, I encourage the person to imagine themself carrying out a behavioural task before doing so and again help them to see that this is a portable skill that they can use whenever relevant.

Repeated practice of attitude–behaviour consistency. While attitude change can happen quickly, most of the time it happens more gradually, and the best way that the volunteer can promote their attitude change is to apply repeatedly a principle that I call attitude–behaviour consistency. This means that if the person wants to internalise a flexible or non-extreme attitude towards an adversity, then they need to think and act in ways that are internally consistent in the face of the adversity and do so over a period until their attitude changes. To do this, they need to recognise the ways that they may use to keep themself safe or comfortable in the short term that interfere with the process of attitude change in the longer term and to refrain from using their safety-seeking manoeuvres. All I can do in a VBTC is to introduce the concept of the repeated practice of attitude–behaviour consistency and help the person to plan to apply it.

Examining and changing inferences. I mentioned earlier that once I have helped the volunteer to identify the adversity at 'A'. I encourage them to assume temporarily that it is true. However, sometimes the volunteer is more keen to change 'A' then to assume that it is true and use it as a route to identify 'B'. Given this, and in order to maintain a good alliance with the person, I will help them to stand back and question the validity of their inference at 'A'.

When I help the volunteer examine their inference, I ask them to focus on the situation they were in and then ask them if their 'A' was the most realistic way of viewing the situation given all the evidence to hand. This involves considering the inference that they made, considering alternative inferences, evaluating all the possibilities and choosing the most realistic inference. Here is a list of other questions that I use when helping the volunteer to examine 'A':

- How likely is it that 'A' happened (or might happen)?
- Would an objective jury agree that 'A' happened or might happen? If not, what would the jury's verdict be?
- Did you view (are you viewing) the situation realistically? If not, how could you have viewed (can you view) it more realistically?
- If you asked someone who you can trust to give you an objective opinion about the truth or falsity of your inference about the situation at hand, what would the person say to you and why? How would this person encourage you to view the situation instead?
- If a friend had told you that they had faced the same situation as you faced and had made the same inference, what would you say to them about the validity of their inference and why? How would you encourage the person to view the situation instead?

Once the person has changed their inference, I suggest that they can use the same method of questioning inferences for themselves whenever they need to do so.

Changing behaviour. Again, given the very brief nature of a VBTC, the input I can have in helping the volunteer to change their behaviour is limited. However, there are a few things I can do.

Change own behaviour to promote desired change in others. A common problem for which a volunteer seeks help is difficulty with another person's behaviour. In such circumstances, I can help the person in two ways. First, as already discussed, if the person is disturbed about the other's behaviour, I can help them to undisturb themself. Then I can discuss how best to influence the other person to change. This is best done if the volunteer considers how their behaviour may be unwittingly perpetuating the other person's behaviour. This can be assessed in the session through conversation or through role-playing where I give them feedback on how they are acting. Then they can consider alternative behaviours and their likely impacts on the behaviour of the other. Once they have decided how to change their behaviour, I may again set up a role-play to give them an opportunity to practise it and see how it feels.

Skills training. Occasionally it becomes apparent that at the heart of the volunteer's problem is a lack of skilful execution of an important behaviour and it is clear that the person does not have a complicating emotional problem. A common example of this is assertiveness. I will assess the person's skill here through role-playing as before and give feedback to shape the person's skill through repeated role-played practice.

Using behaviour to examine inferences. In a previous section, I discussed how I help a volunteer to stand back and examine a distorted inference at 'A'. The methods that I outlined were 'cognitive' in nature. The person can also use behaviour to examine distorted inferences, and when they do this, these are known as 'behavioural experiments'. These experiments may be developed to test inferences about the behaviour of others (a specific person or a group of people where surveys may be constructed and carried out) or about one's own behaviour (e.g. 'if I move out of my safety zone, I will pass out').

Here are guidelines that I employ in helping a volunteer construct a behavioural experiment:

1. I help the person to make a specific prediction.
2. I help the person to design an experiment to test the prediction. I encourage them to be as specific as possible concerning behaviour, time and setting. For it to be a fair test, they need to identify their safety-seeking manoeuvres and resolve not to use them.
3. When they carry out the experiment, they should record what they observe.
4. I then encourage them to reflect on their observations concerning their original prediction and to come up with a different inference that might account better for the data.

The important point that my volunteer and I need to keep in mind is that we will not be able to discuss the results of the behavioural experiment given the 'one-off' nature of a VBTC. This, of course, would not be the case in ongoing therapy.

Chunking behaviour. In constructing a complex behavioural task, it is clear that the person may benefit from breaking the task down into manageable chunks so that they don't get overwhelmed by the task and have a plan that they can follow. This can also be useful in dealing with problems of procrastination where the person has a lot of work to catch up with.

The importance of rewarding behaviour. Sometimes it becomes apparent that the volunteer can benefit from rewarding behaviour that they would like to increase either in themself or another person. A simple reminder of one of the basic principles of psychology can sometimes solve a previously intractable problem.

Acceptance-based strategies

One the major recent developments within the CBT tradition has been the growth of those CBT approaches that recommend that clients mindfully accept the presence of dysfunctional cognitions and troublesome feelings without engaging with them (see Harris, 2009). This may be thought of as an acceptance-based focus and is typical of what has become known as 'third-wave' CBT. My practice in VBTCs is informed mostly, but not exclusively, by REBT (a 'second-wave' CBT approach). Using this approach, I would encourage a volunteer to identify, challenge and change their rigid and extreme attitudes (at 'B') in the Situational ABC framework and respond to distorted inferences (mainly at 'A' or at 'C'). In short, I try to help my volunteer to engage mindfully with troublesome cognitions (i.e. inferences and beliefs) with the purpose of changing them. This represents a change-based focus in VBTC.

As I said at the outset, my approach to VBTCs is pluralistic, and I think both/and rather than either/or when it comes to these two foci. Here is how I make use of both a change-based focus, where attitudes and inferences are targeted for change, and an acceptance-based focus, where these cognitions are mindfully accepted.

I use a change-based focus when inviting a volunteer to examine their rigid/flexible and extreme/non-extreme attitudes or distorted inferences. I also encourage them to use this focus for themself after the VBTC has been completed. But when they consider that they have got enough out of this focus as they can on any particular occasion, I encourage them to shift to an acceptance-based focus if the troublesome attitude or inference is still in their mind. It is unrealistic to expect a person to be convinced fully of their change-based focus interventions in any single disputing episode.

With highly distorted cognitive consequences of rigid and extreme attitudes, I initially teach a volunteer to understand why these thoughts are so distorted (i.e. they are the product of a rigid and extreme attitude). I then help them to use the presence of these thoughts to identify the rigid or extreme attitude that has spawned them and then to use a change-based focus with this attitude. If I have time, I may then help the person to use a change-based focus to respond to these cognitive 'C's, but to recognise again that as these thoughts may still reverberate in their mind, they should at this point switch to an acceptance-based focus. Such reverberation is a natural process as the mind does not switch off from such thoughts just because change-based focus methods have been successfully used on any one occasion.

As third-wave CBT therapists note, little productive change can be gained when a person becomes enmeshed and entwined with their rigid and extreme attitudes and distorted inferences, and it is then when I advocate the use of an acceptance-based focus. However, little can be gained by failing to encourage a volunteer to respond constructively to these cognitions by employing a change-based focus when they can do so.

Bringing the conversation to a suitable end

As I have mentioned throughout this book, VBTCs are time-limited conversations that occur in a public context where my main objectives are to help the volunteer and to educate the audience. However, my main allegiance is to the volunteer who has taken the courageous step to discuss a personal problem in front of an audience. Given this allegiance, I take it upon myself to bring the conversation to a suitable conclusion. I may do this before the 30 minutes has elapsed. Indeed, an analysis of 245 VBTCs that I have conducted showed that the mean length of a conversation is 20 minutes and 11 seconds. Remember that I am guided by the principle of 'one thing', so when it appears to me that the person has gotten that one thing from our conversation, I bring it to a close and then call upon the audience to ask the volunteer and me questions.

In the next chapter, I will consider and discuss the kinds of issues people raise when volunteering for a VBTC.

Notes

1 When referring to a meta-problem, I call the initial problem the 'primary problem'. For this reason, some REB therapists refer to what I am calling a 'meta-problem' as a 'secondary problem'.
2 Known as 'Clue' in North America.
3 The reason why a volunteer may reveal a highly distorted inference at 'C' rather than the adversity at 'A' is because my questioning has led them to access their rigid and extreme attitudes (at 'B'), which leads to them focusing on the highly distorted products of these attitudes.

4 I have constructed the dialogues here between myself and Don to exemplify the points made in the chapter.

5 Thus, when appropriate, I use the 'WRAP' method to help the person differentiate between: (i) their awfulising attitude versus their non-awfulising attitude; (ii) their discomfort intolerance attitude versus their discomfort tolerance attitude; or (iii) their devaluation attitude versus their acceptance attitude.

6 While my remarks largely concern examining rigid and flexible attitudes with a view to changing the former to the latter, they equally apply to examining extreme and non-extreme attitudes, again with a view to changing the former to the latter.

Chapter 6

What volunteers discuss in VBTCs and my approach to these issues

Introduction

In Part 2 of this book, I will present and discuss the verbatim transcripts of several VBTCs that I have had with volunteers over the years that I have been conducting these public conversations. Before I do so, in this chapter, I will present information concerning the issues that people raise when volunteering to have a conversation with me in front of an audience. I will consider the most commonly presented issues and discuss how I tend to conceptualise and address them and the key learnings that I hope that volunteers will take away with them from talking to me about these issues.

Let me stress at the outset that while I will concentrate on my way of conceptualising and responding to the issues that volunteers raise in VBTCs, in practice, I also place much emphasis on their views of their issues and how they can best be helped, and I incorporate these during our discussions.

The context

Before I present information about the 245 volunteers with whom I have had therapeutic conversations, let me say a little about the context of these conversations. I normally like to give a live demonstration of the way I work whenever I talk about a therapeutic subject because it helps the process come alive for the audience and it gives the volunteers an opportunity to get some help on whatever issues they are troubled about. In the setting in which most of the 245 conversations took place, volunteers could have 'carte blanche' about the problem they wished to raise with me. However, 82 of the 245 conversations (33.5%) took place at the United Kingdom

Cognitive Behaviour Therapy (UKCBT) Meetup group. At these meetings, I first give a lecture on a particular themes and then call for volunteers who have issues consistent with that evening's theme. Please bear this in mind when considering the information that I will provide presently.

The volunteers

It is in the nature of a VBTC that I know nothing about the person before they volunteer and, in the majority of cases. I don't know what, if anything, they have derived from the conversation after it finished. I will discuss the need for research on these conversations in the Afterword. However, let me make a few general observations about the people who volunteer for a VBTC.

It seems to me that people who volunteer for a VBTC tend to have the following characteristics:

- They are bright.
- They are articulate in expressing their problem/issue.
- They process information quite fast.
- They tend to have the confidence to talk about their problems in front of others.
- They tend to be inclined towards or have an interest in CBT.
- Many of the them tend to be helping professionals themselves.
- They tend to be able to trust me very quickly.
- They disclose their problems readily, often at quite a deep level.
- They tend to have a sense of humour.

As may be seen from the above, they bring a number of positive factors to VBTCs that help them get the most out of these conversations.

General observations

Information in this chapter is taken from a sample of 245 volunteers with whom I have had conversations from 2005 to 2017. Of the 245, 192 were women (78.4%) and 53 were men (21.6%). A total of 165 conversations were conducted in the UK (67.3%), 52 in the USA (21.2%) and 28 in the rest of the world[1] (11.5%).

When I send a conversation to be transcribed, I ask the transcriber to identify the major theme of the conversation, which I then verify. For this book, we then grouped the themes by category and

Table 6.1 Themes discussed in VBTCs by category

Theme category	Total
Anxiety and phobia	49
Problems with procrastination	39
Anger problems	27
Self-esteem problems	27
Problems with uncertainty	25
Relationships problems	22
Problems with lack of control	14
Other emotional problems	42
Totals	**245**

this analysis is presented in Table 6.1. This table gives the total for each theme category and shows in decreasing order the frequency with which each category was raised by volunteers.

In the rest of this chapter, I will consider each theme category and show the range of specific themes/issues that occur in each category and how I understand and address them. In doing so, it is my intention to present only the main points that I consider when having a VBTC rather than a comprehensive view of how such problems can be understood and addressed. Also, please bear in mind that my goal is to help the person take away one main thing that may make a meaningful difference to them as they address their problem after the VBTC. My discussion of the main problems raised by volunteers in VBTCs is informed by both of these points.

Anxiety and phobia

As can be seen from Table 6.1, the most commonly raised concern was that of anxiety/phobia, which was discussed in 49 of the total number of 245 conversations (20.0%). Of these 49 people, 42 were women (85.7%) and 7 were men (14.3%). The fact that anxiety was the most common problem is not surprising given that it is one of the two most common problems for which people seek help. When we look a little more closely at this category (see Table 6.2), we find that 'performance anxiety' as a specific issue and 'anxiety' as a general issue are the two most commonly raised issues within this general category.

Table 6.2 Themes raised by volunteers in the theme category: anxiety and phobia

Theme	Number
Performance anxiety	12
Anxiety	11
Phobia	6
Worry	5
Fear	4
Stress	3
Anxiety and guilt	1
Claustrophobia	1
Difficulty with getting lost	1
Problem with meanness	1
Monophobia	1
Overwork	1
Needle phobia	1
Social anxiety	1
Anxiety and phobia: total	**49**

Understanding anxiety

In understanding anxiety, I use the 'ABC' framework that I introduced and discussed in Chapter 3. Here, anxiety is regarded as an emotional 'C' and the adversity at 'A' is an actual or perceived threat to the volunteer's personal domain[2] (Beck, 1976). When a volunteer is anxious about a threat, they hold rigid and extreme attitudes towards that threat and they consider that they would not be able to deal with it if it occurred. My goal, if I can achieve it in the time available to me, is to help them to move towards feeling unanxious concern about the threat. I do this by: (i) helping them to develop flexible and non-extreme attitudes towards the threat; and (ii) helping them to see that they can deal with it if it occurred. Then, I help the person plan to implement this learning in their everyday life.

I sometimes find it useful to suggest to a volunteer that we view their anxiety as a plant and consider the conditions in which this plant would thrive. Later I will help them to identify the conditions in which it would wither.

Here are some of the major conditions that lead anxiety to thrive in the longer term:

- Processing the threat with rigid and extreme attitudes.
- Avoiding the threat.
- Avoiding the anxiety likely to be experienced if facing the threat.
- Thinking that anxiety is intolerable.
- Attempting to eliminate the feelings of anxiety.
- Withdrawing from the threat as quickly as possible.
- Attempting to distract oneself from anxiety.
- Using 'closets'; one of my commonly used phrases is 'anxiety loves closets'.
- Using a variety of safety-seeking manoeuvres (behavioural and cognitive) designed to keep the person safe in the moment from the threat.
- Seeking reassurance from others and oneself.
- Using mood-altering substances (e.g. alcohol, food or drugs).
- Relying on others to protect oneself.
- Changing one's inference at 'A' before one has had the opportunity to face and deal with the adversity.
- Thinking that the highly distorted cognitive consequences of rigid and extreme attitudes are a true guide to the future.

Understanding performance anxiety

As I mentioned above, performance anxiety was the most common specific problem raised by volunteers under the 'anxiety and phobia' category. The threats in such anxiety commonly relate to the person anticipating that:

- They will not live up to their own desired performance standard.
- They will be anxious in the performance situation.
- Others will negatively evaluate them for their 'poor' performance.
- Others will notice and negatively evaluate them for being anxious.
- They will not achieve a prized goal due to their 'poor' performance and/or anxiety display.

The above threats are all placed at 'A' in the 'Situational ABC' framework that I use. What leads the person to be anxious rather than healthily concerned about these threats are the rigid and extreme attitudes that they hold towards these inferred adversities at 'A'. Rather than help the person to consider the likelihood that a threat will occur (e.g. "What is the likelihood that people watching you will notice that you are anxious or evaluate you negatively if they do?"), I encourage them to assume temporarily that their inference is true. I do this as a way of helping them to identify their rigid and/or extreme attitudes towards such an adversity (e.g. "People must not see that I am anxious and think badly of me if they do, and if this happens, I could not bear it"). Commonly used strategies that people use to cope with their performance anxiety that only serve to maintain it include:

- Over-preparation or over-rehearsal to eliminate errors.
- Playing safe instead of taking calculated risks.
- Finding ways of hiding from those watching (e.g. giving a PowerPoint presentation with the lighting dimmed or standing with one's back to the audience).
- Using alcohol or prescription medication to 'control one's nerves'.

Helping the person to deal with anxiety

What are the conditions in which anxiety would wither? Here is a list of the major conditions that can form the basis of a treatment strategy for anxiety:

- Facing a threat and processing it with flexible and non-extreme attitudes.
- Accepting the presence of anxious feelings without liking them and without trying to eliminate them.
- Thinking that anxiety is tolerable and is worth tolerating.
- Actually tolerating the anxiety likely to be experienced if facing the threat.
- Coming out of 'closets'.
- Facing a threat while refraining from using safety-seeking manoeuvres.
- Tolerating uncertainty without reassurance seeking.
- Refraining from using mood-altering substances.
- Relying on oneself for protection.
- Changing one's inference at 'A' after one has had the opportunity to face and deal with the adversity.

- Thinking that the highly distorted cognitive consequences of rigid and extreme attitudes stem from these attitudes and are unlikely to be a true guide to the future.

When having a conversation with a volunteer about their anxiety problem, my goal is to help the person take away at least one of the above helping principles that is most meaningful to them and likely to make the most difference to their life.

Helping the person deal with performance anxiety

Within the context of a VBTC, once I have helped the person with performance anxiety to identify the 'ABC' features of their problem, I encourage them to strive to:

- Question their rigid and/or extreme attitudes towards 'A'.
- Commit to their alternative flexible and/or non-extreme attitudes.
- See that their attitude towards others for flawed performance is more accepting and compassionate than towards their own.
- Adopt a self-compassionate attitude based first on unconditional self-acceptance and identify and deal with DROs to doing so.
- If possible, practise the performance based on the flexible/non-extreme attitudes in the session.
- Rehearse the flawed performance in imagery while holding the flexible and/or non-extreme attitudes.
- Develop a realistic inference at 'A' if distorted.

Problems with procrastination

The second most common problem raised by volunteers was procrastination (see Table 6.1), which featured in 39 of the total number of 245 conversations (15.9%). Of these 39 volunteers, 30 were women (76.9%) and 9 were men (23.1%). While this problem can have a decidedly negative impact on people, it is an issue that people are quite comfortable discussing in public, as it is a universal issue.

Understanding procrastination

When a person procrastinates, they put off doing a task that is in their best interest to do at a time when it is in their best interest to do it. The task and their best interest are judged by the person themself rather than by me as a therapist. I thus see procrastination as avoidant behaviour at 'C' in the 'ABC' framework (Dryden, 2000). Although common, procrastination is difficult to assess because quite often the person does not know what they are avoiding (at 'A') or what their major emotion at 'C' would be if they encountered what they are avoiding.

I have found that when assessing a volunteer's procrastination problem, it is important to ask them to nominate a very specific example and to help the person to be clear the moment that they are procrastinating. Just before they begin to procrastinate, I ask to them identify what they think their emotional 'C' would be and I use that to identify the 'A'. Common 'C's are anxiety and unhealthy anger. The reason the person procrastinates is not that they might encounter the 'A', but because of the rigid and extreme attitudes that they hold about the 'A'.

Alternatively, I ask the person what condition they think they need to have in order to begin a task. The opposite of this is the adversity that they seek to avoid. This is a version of the 'Windy's Magic Question' method that I presented in Box 5.1. Table 6.3 outlines the ABC framework of procrastination with examples of common adversities and associated rigid attitudes.

Helping the person to deal with procrastination

In Table 6.3, I also present the flexible attitudes towards the same adversities the person would need to hold to overcome their procrastination problem. The development of such attitudes is the cornerstone of the person addressing their procrastination effectively. Also, the following points are important for the person to consider:

- The development of an attitude of discomfort tolerance is generally important in overcoming procrastination.
- The volunteer's worth as a person is fixed and not determined by achievement or performance.
- The volunteer can get a sense of freedom by choosing to do something unpleasant that they are told to do if it is in their interest to do so rather than rebelling against the other person by not doing it.
- The volunteer needs to identify and respond to rationalisations that intend to show themself and/or others that they are not procrastinating when they are.

Table 6.3 The ABCs of 'procrastination' and 'taking timely action'

'A'	'B'	'C'
Being uncomfortable while doing the task	"I must be comfortable before I start the task" "I would like to be comfortable before I start the task, but this condition isn't necessary"	Procrastination until comfortable Start the task even though uncomfortable
Not being in the mood to do the task	"I must be in the mood before I start the task" "I would like to be in the mood before I start the task, but this condition isn't necessary"	Procrastination on the task until in the mood Start the task even though not in the mood
Not 'feeling' competent to do the task	"I must feel competent before I start the task" "I would like to feel competent before I start the task, but this condition isn't necessary"	Procrastination on the task until the feeling of competence is experienced Start the task even though not feeling competent
Not being motivated to do the task	"I must be motivated before I start the task" "I would like to be motivated before I start the task, but this condition isn't necessary"	Procrastination on the task until motivated Start the task even though not motivated
Immediate understanding	"I must understand what I have to do before I start to do it" "I would like to understand what I have to do before I start to do it, but this condition isn't necessary"	Procrastination on the task until understanding has been obtained Start the task even though lacking understanding of what to do

Table 6.3 (Cont.)

'A'	'B'	'C'
Pressure	"I must be under pressure before I start the task" "While I might like to be under pressure before I start work, this condition isn't necessary"	Procrastination on the task until under pressure Start work even though not under pressure
Immediate gratification	"Faced with the choice of doing something that I enjoy or starting the task, I must do what I want to do" "Faced with the choice of doing something that I enjoy or starting the task, I would like to do what I want, but this condition isn't necessary"	Procrastination on the task until immediately gratified Start the task foregoing immediate gratification

- The person needs to develop healthy attitudes towards procrastination-related adversities *before* they use a variety of practical steps to help in overcoming procrastination.
- Once the person has developed a healthy attitude, then the following practical steps can be helpful in addressing procrastination:
  - Setting work-based goals and being goal-focused.
  - Developing better self-discipline routines.
  - Improving management of time.
  - Choosing the best working environment.
  - Improving task skills.
  - Reinforcing task behaviour.
  - Chunking periods when doing the task and taking suitable breaks without returning to procrastination behaviour.
  - Getting exercise and developing good nutritional habits to protect from lethargy.
  - Getting a good night's sleep to keep one fresh for the task work.

- I will draw upon the above methods instead of focusing on attitudes at 'B' when the person does not resonate with the idea of developing a healthy set of adversity-related attitudes or is disinclined to do so.

Anger problems

The joint third most common problem raised by volunteers was anger (see Table 6.1), which featured in 27 of the total number of 245 conversations (11.1%). Of these 38 volunteers, 18 were women (66.7%) and 9 were men (33.3%).

Understanding problematic anger

Whenever a volunteer wishes to discuss an anger problem with me, my first concern is to ascertain whether their anger is healthy or unhealthy.

Distinguishing between healthy and unhealthy anger

I do this by asking the person their view on the constructiveness of their anger and, if necessary, I outline the main behaviours and action tendencies associated with unhealthy anger and healthy anger to see if this helps clarify the issue for the person (see Appendix 1).

Identifying rigid and extreme attitudes

The same inferences are found in healthy and unhealthy anger. These inferences include frustration, goal obstruction, bad treatment from another, rule transgression by other(s) or self and someone devaluing or disrespecting self. So, these do not differentiate unhealthy from healthy anger (at 'C'). What does are the attitudes (at 'B') that the person holds towards the inferences at 'A', with rigid and extreme attitudes underpinning unhealthy anger and flexible and non-extreme attitudes underpinning healthy anger. Thus, I need to help the person see the relationship between their unhealthy anger and the rigid and extreme attitudes that they hold towards the inference at 'A'.

Also, I am guided by three important principles when striving to understand a volunteer's anger problem:

Identify the short-term and longer-term consequences of the person's unhealthy anger. My experience is that the person may see the short-term consequences of their unhealthy anger as positive. They may 'feel' powerful, for example, and if expressed, such anger may result in the person getting what they want. However, the longer-term consequences are largely negative. They alienate those on the receiving end of their anger, who may wish to get even with them or feel intimidated by the person and seek to avoid them. Thus, unhealthy anger leads to the deterioration and the eventual dissolution of valued relationships.

Discover DROs the person may have to relinquish their unhealthy anger. I need to discover these and help the person to question them. Otherwise, they will act as a restraining force as I strive to help the person to move towards developing healthy anger. For example, some people think that their unhealthy anger is evidence that they are correct in the views that they hold. It is my job to question such a misconception and show them that they can be correct when both healthily angry and unhealthily angry, but unhealthy anger indicates that they are rigid and dogmatic about being correct.

Identify unhealthy anger ruminations. Here, the question is: does the person ruminate when unhealthily angry or not and, if so, what is the content of their ruminations? Angry fantasies, when anger is unhealthy, are often ruminative and provide the person with pleasure and/or with a sense of power when they picture themself taking revenge on the other person, sometimes in quite violent ways. If the person in reality feels powerless, then they are often resistant to letting go of their angry fantasies unless I can help them gain a sense of power in real life.

Helping the person deal with problematic anger

Helping the person deal with their problematic anger involves me dealing with several important issues. Of course, in 30 minutes I do not have the time to deal with all of these issues, but I list them all here to show the range of issues that I can highlight with the volunteer's active involvement.

Constructing healthy anger responses

Once the person has agreed that their anger is problematic and they wish to change it, it is important that I work with them to construct a viable, healthy alternative that can serve as their goal. This involves me helping them to do the following:

- Construct functional behavioural responses to the inference at 'A'.
- See that these behavioural responses have more beneficial longer-term consequences for them than the behaviour associated with their unhealthy anger.
- Encourage them to discover short-term benefits of their healthy anger and to tolerate the deprivation of the short-term pleasure and/or power of their unhealthy anger.
- Construct non-ruminative cognitive concomitants of healthy anger.

Developing flexible and non-extreme attitudes

In my view, the development of flexible and non-extreme attitudes towards anger-related inferences at 'A' is the key to helping a volunteer deal with their anger problem in the long-term. In particular, since rigidity is at the heart of problematic anger, in my view, I place a lot of attention on the importance of developing flexibility in the time I have with the volunteer as long as they resonate with this concept. Otherwise, I will highlight the development of other-acceptance in other-directed anger or self-acceptance in ego-defensive anger (see the 'Self-esteem problems' section later in this chapter).

Promoting inference change, if necessary

If I am not making progress with encouraging attitude change, I will encourage inference change in the volunteer. This means that while their rigid and extreme attitudes remain in place, helping them to see that they were incorrect in making the anger-related inference and to make a more benign inference means that these attitudes are deactivated. The problem with this approach is that these rigid and extreme attitudes may be reactivated later when the person makes another anger-related inference.

For example, I remember my friend and colleague, Richard Wessler, telling me the following story concerning the wisdom of promoting inference change when attitude change proved not to be possible. Richard was working with a middle-aged married woman who reported feeling furious every time her ageing father would telephone her and enquire, "Noo, what's doing?" She inferred that this was a gross invasion of her privacy and dogmatically insisted that he had no right to do so. Richard initially intervened by attempting to dispute this client's rigid attitude and tried to help her see that there was no law in the universe that stated that her father must not do such a thing. Meeting initial resistance, he persisted with different variations of this theme, all to no avail. Changing tack, Richard began to implement a different strategy designed to help the client question her inference that her father was invading her privacy. Given her father's age, Richard enquired, was it not more likely that his question represented his usual manner of beginning telephone conversations rather than an intense desire to pry into her affairs? This enquiry proved successful in that the client's rage subsided because she began to reinterpret her father's motives. Interestingly enough, although Richard returned to question her rigid attitude later, he never succeeded in helping this client to develop a flexible attitude about inferred parental invasion of her privacy!

Teaching and refining assertiveness skills

When I am discussing unhealthy interpersonal anger with the volunteer, once I have helped them to develop a flexible and/or other-accepting attitude towards the other person, and if I have sufficient time, I will focus on the topic of assertiveness. Thus, I may assess their assertiveness skills through role play and teach them skills that are not already in their repertoire and help them to refine their existing skills. Occasionally, I may highlight assertiveness, particularly if the person is interested in neither attitude change nor inference change.

Teaching mindfulness skills

When dealing with angry ruminations, I suggest first that the person looks for the rigid attitude that drives their ruminations, then that they examine this attitude and finally that they develop and commit to the flexible alternative. Then I suggest that they notice their angry ruminations and neither engage with them nor try to eliminate them. I do this using one of the metaphors that stem from 'acceptance and commitment therapy' (e.g. the 'passengers on the bus' metaphor[3] – see Hayes, Strosahl & Wilson, 2012).

Self-esteem problems

What was surprising to me was that depression did not feature as a category in the analysis of 245 volunteers. My view on this is that people who are depressed present by discussing the issue/theme about which they are depressed. When they do so, their feelings of depression are not to the fore and thus it does not feature as a theme category. One major theme that volunteers did bring to the VBTC context that is relevant to depression is self-esteem issues.

As can be seen from Table 6.1, the joint third most commonly raised issue concerned problems to do with low self-esteem, which was discussed in 27 of the total number of 245 conversations (11.0%). Of these 27 people, 23 were women (85.2%) and 4 were men (14.8%). When we look a little more closely at this category (see Table 6.4), we see that volunteers express self-esteem problems in several different ways and that these problems feature in several different contexts. Also, it should be borne in mind that self-esteem issues also feature in other problems raised by volunteers. However, the theme emphasised by these volunteers did not mention low self-esteem by name and was thus otherwise categorised.

Table 6.4 Themes raised by volunteers in the theme category: low self-esteem

Theme	Number
Lack of self-worth	7
Lack of self-acceptance	5
Low self-esteem	4
Self-hatred	2
Difficulty with lack of approval	2
Difficulty with failure	2
Problem in dealing with abuse	1
Difficulty with assertion	1
Lack of self-confidence	1
Self-doubt	1
Self-criticism	1
Low self-esteem: total	**27**

Understanding self-esteem problems

Self-esteem problems can be found in most, if not all, of the eight major emotional problems for which people seek help: anxiety, depression, guilt, shame, hurt, ego-defensive anger, jealousy and envy. I tend to use the ABC framework outlined in Chapter 3 in understanding the volunteer's self-esteem problem. Working with a specific example of the person's self-esteem problem, I would begin with 'C', which would be one of the eight emotions listed above. Then, I would use the selected 'C' to identify 'A', which would be the aspect of the situation about which the person would be most disturbed. Then I would help the person identify both the rigid and self-devaluation attitudes that account for the problem.

When identifying the person's self-devaluation attitude, it is important to use the person's self-devaluing language. I encourage the person to be as honest as they can be about such language, especially if it is profane and may be distasteful to the observing audience. When the person's undiluted, self-devaluing language is used in a VBTC, they are more likely to connect emotionally to the conversation than when their language is sanitised and changed.

Dealing with self-esteem problems

In dealing with self-esteem problems, my main goal is to help the person construct, commit to and see how they can implement a healthy alternative to the self-devaluation attitude that accounts for their problem. Theoretically, this attitude is known as 'unconditional self-acceptance'. In doing so, I am guided by several principles.

Goal setting

As with other problems, it is important that I help the person to set realistic goals for their self-esteem problem once we have assessed the problem.

Promoting attitudinal choice

In the assessment phase, I would have helped the person to identify their self-devaluation attitude. If I did not also help them to develop their alternative unconditional self-acceptance (USA) attitude, I would do so now before discussing their basic choice. I explain that no matter how understandable it is for the person to have developed their self-devaluation attitude in the past, they are unwittingly maintaining it both cognitively and behaviourally in the present. They can choose now to develop a 'USA' attitude or to continue to operate on their self-devaluation attitude.

Examining self-devaluation and self-acceptance attitudes

Once the person has chosen to develop a 'USA' attitude, I engage them in an examination of the two attitudes. During this examination process, where I normally invite the person to consider and compare both attitudes at the same time, I seek to make one or more of the following points[4]:

- The self (or person) is too complex to be given a legitimate, global rating. The person makes such a negative evaluation when they devaluate themselves.
- The self (or person) cannot be defined by any aspect. A visual representation of this point is 'i ≠ I'. This means that the self (or 'big I') cannot be defined by one of its aspects (or 'little i'). This is known as the 'big I – little i' technique. If a person resonates with this equation, I suggest that they write it down and consult it regularly.
- The essence of USA is unconditionality. Thus, self-acceptance can be adopted without conditions attached. I joking refer to this as 'NSA-SA' (literally 'no strings attached self-acceptance').
- If the person wishes to esteem themself, then the healthiest way of doing so is unconditionally. I call this 'unconditional self-esteem'. Here the person, in effect, says that they are worthwhile because they are human, fallible, complex, unique, in flux and alive and nothing can take their worth as a person away from them unless they choose to do so.

Deepening conviction in the 'USA' attitude

Once the person has understood their 'USA' attitude and its pragmatic value, truth and logic, it is important that I help them to begin the process of deepening their conviction in this attitude. In the session, I may set up a two-chair dialogue between the person's self-devaluation attitude and 'USA' attitude with the purpose of having the person respond to points made by the part of them that holds the former attitude (Kellogg, 2015). Between sessions, I encourage the person to act in ways that are consistent with their 'USA' attitude and to do so regularly.

Planning to act and rehearsal

With deepening conviction in their 'USA' attitude in mind, I help the person to develop an action plan and encourage them to see themself in their mind's eye acting in a way that is consistent with this attitude while rehearsing a short-hand, memorable version of it.

Dealing with DROs to attitudinal change

Sometimes a volunteer may show reluctance in changing their self-devaluation attitude to a 'USA' attitude, in which case it is important for me to identify and respond to any DROs that the person has concerning letting go of their self-devaluation attitude and developing their 'USA' attitude.

Incorporating mindfulness strategies

Once a volunteer has engaged in a period of examining their self-devaluation and 'USA' attitudes and committed to the latter, the former attitude and its cognitive referents may still be in the person's mind. Rather than continuing to examine or question it, I recommend that the person adopts a mindful stance to such attitudes and thoughts. This involves the person acknowledging the continuing existence of such cognitions without re-engaging with them or attempting to ignore or eliminate them. I explain that adopting this mindful stance is akin to a taking a break after the person has exercised in the gym. It is to enable the person to take a break from cognitive change until they can benefit from another attitude examination period.

Problems with uncertainty

The fifth most common problem raised by volunteers was uncertainty (see Table 6.1), which featured in 25 of the total number of 245 conversations (10.2%). Of these 25 volunteers, 19 were women (76.0%) and 6 were men (24.0%). When we look a little more closely at this category (see Table 6.5), we find that 'problem with uncertainty'

Table 6.5 Themes raised by volunteers in the theme category: problems with uncertainty

Theme	Number
Difficulty with uncertainty	8
Difficulty with decision-making	6
Difficulty with commitment	2
Certainty issues	1
Difficulty with perfectionism	1
Difficulty moving on	1
Problems with uncertainty: total	**19**

as a general issue and 'difficulty with decision-making' as a specific issue were the two most commonly raised issues within this general category.

Understanding problems with uncertainty

As with other issues, when I strive to understand a volunteer's problem with uncertainty, I first ask for a specific example and use the 'Situational ABC' framework to help me. In doing so, I am guided by several principles.

Uncertainty is linked to another inference

People don't disturb themselves about uncertainty in general, but rather when uncertainty is related to another specific issue that they find problematic. For example, in health anxiety, the person is anxious about uncertainty related to illness, and in decision-making anxiety, they are anxious about uncertainty concerning making the 'wrong' decision. In these scenarios, then, 'illness' and the 'wrong' decision are what I call 'linked inferences'. Thus, I strive to understand what the volunteer's linked inference is when they are having a problem with uncertainty.

Rigidity is the problem

To paraphrase Epictetus, people are disturbed not by uncertainty, but by their rigid attitude towards uncertainty. Thus, I look for the person's rigid attitude and help them to understand the core role that it plays in their uncertainty-related problem.

Using the quadrant approach in assessment

I devised the quadrant approach to help me to understand how a person thinks when facing uncertainty in a key area of their life, such as health/illness (see Table 6.6). In quadrants 1 and 2, the person has certainty. They know that they are well (quadrant 1) or ill (quadrant 2). For our purposes, we can put these quadrants aside. Quadrants 3 and 4 are more relevant as the person is in a state of uncertainty. In quadrant 3, they think that they are probably well, while in quadrant 4, they think that they are ill. When a person has health anxiety, uncertainty is an adversity for them towards which they hold a rigid attitude (e.g. "I must know that I am well and as I don't know this then I am ill"). Thus, they live in quadrant 4. As they can't convince themself that they are well (quadrant 1), they therefore think that they are ill. Put simply, uncertainty equals illness. I will return to the quadrant approach when discussing how to deal with problems with uncertainty.

Table 6.6 The quadrant approach

	Well	Ill
Certain	1	2
Uncertain	3	4

Quadrant 1: The person knows that they are well.
Quadrant 2: The person knows that they are ill.
Quadrant 3: The person is in a state of uncertainty, but thinks that they are probably well.
Quadrant 4: The person is in a state of uncertainty, but thinks that they are ill.

Being certain versus feeling certain

For some people with difficulties with uncertainty, it is 'being certain' that is the important desired ingredient. Such people are comforted, for example, with being told by an expert that they are well (to use the example of health anxiety). For others, the desired ingredient is the more experiential 'feeling certain'. Such people are comforted when they have this 'experiential' sense of certainty. I find it useful to discover which type of certainty the person is seeking.

What the person does to gain a sense of certainty

One of the ways in which the volunteer maintains their problem with uncertainty is what they do to gain actual and/or experiential certainty. In particular, I am interested in both overt and implicit attempts to gain reassurance from another person.

Uncertainty and 'doing nothing'

Often people who have a problem with uncertainty try to solve the problem by doing nothing. This is particularly the case with those who experience problems making decisions. If this is the case, I want to discover what the person hopes to achieve by inaction and what it actually achieves.

Dealing with problems with uncertainty

When helping a volunteer with their problem with uncertainty, I am guided by the following principles.

Set goals

As with other problems, it is important that I help the person set realistic goals. While usually the person wants to solve their problem with uncertainty by becoming certain, the truth is that this will only serve to maintain the problem. My task is to help them to move forward in life while being or feeling uncertain. Once the person has set a goal, I encourage them to commit to going forward according to probability rather than certainty.

Help change attitudes towards uncertainty and the linked inference

As uncertainty is only really problematic when attached to a linked inference, I need to promote attitude change towards the uncertainty-linked inference pairing. For example, if the volunteer's rigid attitude is "I must know that this mole is benign," then I will help them to change it to a flexible alternative: "I would like to know that this mole is benign, but I don't need to know this."

Living in quadrant 3

In Table 6.6, I outlined the quadrant approach to understanding a person's possible ways of dealing with certainty and uncertainty in the face of adversity. Once I have helped them to develop a flexible attitude to uncertainty in the context of their linked inference (e.g. ill health), I encourage them to live in quadrant 3 (e.g. the person is in a state of uncertainty, but thinks that they are probably well). This involves the person acting in ways that reinforce their flexible attitude and acknowledging their tendency to act in ways that maintain their rigid attitude, but refraining from doing so.

Using mindfulness strategies

Rehearsing and acting on a flexible attitude is crucial in dealing with uncertainty concerning the linked inference. However, it does mean that the person will cease thinking about certainty and how to get it. The mind does not have an on–off switch. Given this, it is important that I help the volunteer to see that the best way to deal with such residual thoughts is to accept them mindfully without re-engaging with them or attempting to eliminate them (see Note 3).

Relationship problems

As can be seen from Table 6.1, the sixth most commonly raised issue concerned relationship problems, which were discussed in 22 of the total number of 245 conversations (9.0%). Of these 22 people, 17 were women (77.3%) and 5 were men (22.7%).

When we look a little more closely at this category (see Table 6.7), we see that volunteers express relationship problems quite generally, but when they do specify them, they mention themes such as problems with rejection, attachment and friendships and difficulties

Table 6.7 Themes raised by volunteers in the theme category: relationship problems

Theme	Number
Relationship problems (general)	11
Problems with rejection	4
Attachment problems	2
Friendship problems	2
Difficulty with boredom	1
Difficulty with caring	1
Difficulty with compassion	1
Relationships problems: total	**22**

with boredom, caring and compassion. Also, it should be borne in mind that relationship issues also feature in other problems raised by volunteers. However, the theme emphasised by these volunteers did not mention relationship problems by name and was thus otherwise categorised.

Understanding relationship problems

When a volunteer raises a relationship problem, my assessment focuses on two questions: (1) is the person emotionally disturbed about the relationship issue? And (2) are they acting in ways that unwittingly maintain the problem?

All eight emotional problems that people seek help with in VBTCs are involved in their relationship problems: anxiety, depression, guilt, shame, hurt, unhealthy forms of anger, jealousy and envy. When the person is emotionally disturbed, then I first present a rationale as to why we should target this intrapersonal problem for change before considering what we can do about the interpersonal problem. If the person agrees, then I will use the 'Situational ABC' framework to assess the problem. If the person does not agree, then I will bypass the intrapersonal problem and focus on the interpersonal problem.

When the volunteer and I focus on the interpersonal nature of the relationship problem, then I will use a specific example to determine what the person is unwittingly doing to maintain the problem.

Dealing with relationship problems

When the person and I have agreed to target their intrapersonal problem first, then I will encourage them to set an appropriate emotional goal. This will help them to consider how they might change their behaviour towards the other person (see below). Once the person has set such a goal, I will help them to develop a flexible and/ or non-extreme attitude towards the adversity about which they are disturbed, which will help them to achieve this goal.

Once I have done this, I will then help the person to determine what change in the other person's behaviour they are seeking. Once they are clear about this, I will encourage them to think about how they might change their behaviour to best influence the other person to change theirs in the desired manner. If I have time, I will use role play to give them an opportunity to practice this behavioural change with me in the role of the other. Before finishing the conversation, if necessary, I will help the person to realise that while they may want the other person to change, sadly they don't have to do so even if the person changes their behaviour.

Problems with lack of control

The smallest problem category raised by volunteers was lack of control (see Table 6.1), which featured in 14 of the total number of 245 conversations (5.7%). Of these 14 volunteers, 12 were women (85.7%) and 2 were men (14.3%). When we look a little more closely at this category (see Table 6.8), we find that problems with lack of self-control and lack of self-discipline were the two most commonly raised issues within this general category.

Understanding problems with lack of control

When a volunteer raises a problem with lack of control, it is usually about self-control. Such a problem may concern their difficulty with stopping something that they are doing that gives them short-term pleasure, relief or feeling but is problematic for them in the longer term. Alternatively, their difficulty is with starting and/or maintaining something that it is in their long-term best interests to do. Let me briefly deal with each issue separately.

Table 6.8 Themes raised by volunteers in the theme category: problems with lack of control

Theme	Number
Problem with lack of self-control	3
Problem with lack of self-discipline	3
Problem with lack of control	2
Problem with alcohol	1
Difficulty with deprivation	1
Problem with gambling	1
Problem with lack of harmony	1
Problem with lateness	1
Difficulty with weight loss	1
Problems with lack of control: total	**14**

Difficulty stopping

When I am working on a volunteer's self-control problem that centres on their difficulty with stopping, I find it useful to distinguish between stopping an internal experience (such as a thought, feeling or urge to act) and an external behaviour.

Stopping an internal experience. Paradoxically, if a person wishes to stop an experience, they will achieve the opposite (i.e. their experience will remain or intensify). If the person were to adopt a rigid attitude towards controlling an internal experience by attempting to stop or eliminate it, then that experience will intensify, which results in the person inferring and fearing that they will lose self-control totally. Their rigid attitude towards self-control thus creates a black and white mental category: 'in control–out of control'. When the person acts on this rigid attitude and black and white categorisation, they may avoid situations where they may experience the internal thoughts, feelings and/or sensations that they wish to stop. This only serves to perpetuate the problem.

Stopping an external behaviour. Gaining control of a behaviour that the person wants to stop tends not to have the paradoxical element that attempting to control internal experience has. When understanding and helping the volunteer to understand this situation, I want to find out the following:

- Is the behaviour connected to an emotion or other internal experience? If so, is it the behavioural expression of an emotion/experience or is it designed to get rid of the emotion/ experience?
- Can the person identify the urge to act that they convert to overt behaviour?
- If so, can they see that they have a choice to act on this urge or not to act on it?
- What is the purposive nature of the behaviour? Put differently, what does the person hope to gain from the behaviour?
- What are the short-term and long-term consequences of the behaviour?
- Can the person see the mismatch between what they hope to gain from the behaviour and what they actually achieve by carrying it out?
- What alternative behaviours are possible?

Difficulty starting and/or maintaining

When a volunteer experiences problems with self-control in the 'difficulty starting/maintaining' area, then they often have difficulties with procrastination (see 'Problems with procrastination' section above) or with implementing a healthy behavioural regime. Usually, the person is waiting for a set of conditions to exist before they implement the behaviour (see Table 6.3, which focuses on procrastination, but has broader relevance). It is important that I help both the volunteer and myself understand what these conditions are. Also, I want to see how the person is construing the regime to which they claim they are committed. What DROs do they have that are important for us both to understand here?

Difficulties with stopping and starting/maintaining often go together

Although I have dealt with both types of difficulties with self-control separately, in reality, they often occur together. Thus, for example, a person may spend too much time playing the slot machines instead of working on their thesis. Ideally, when this is the case, I would like to help the person deal with both difficulties. However, this may not be possible within the time constraints of a VBTC and so I begin by asking the person to select one area to discuss if we only have the time to deal with one. I do stress, though, that I will endeavour to cover both areas, if possible.

Dealing with problems with lack of control

I will consider my approach to dealing with problems with lack of control using the same schema as above.

When the person wants to stop an internal experience

When helping the volunteer address their problem with lack of control of their internal experience, I do the following: first, I help them to acknowledge their desire, but encourage them to develop a flexible attitude (e.g. "I would prefer not to have this thought, but that does not mean that I must not have it"). Second, I help them to understand that to act on their desire is counterproductive and the best way to deal with an wanted thought is to acknowledge its presence, dislike it and neither engage with it nor try to eliminate it. Third, I encourage them to do whatever they would do if they did not have the thought.

When the person wants to stop an undesired behaviour

When helping a volunteer to address their unwanted behaviour when this behaviour is designed to get rid of emotion, I do the following: first, I help them deal with their emotional problem before focusing on the behaviour itself. Second, whether or not the behaviour is connected to emotion, I help the person to recognise that even though they have an urge to act in a certain way, they do not have to act on that urge. They have a choice, and they can choose to act more functionally. Part of this process involves me helping the person to understand one of two points: (a) their problematic behaviour probably does not achieve what they think it will achieve; and (b) even if the problematic behaviour does achieve what they want it to achieve, it probably does not help them in the longer term. At this point, I will encourage them to select behaviour that will satisfy their healthy long-term goals and to commit to implementing such behaviour regularly.

When the person wants to initiate and/or maintain desired behaviour

My major tasks when helping the person to initiate and/or maintain desired behaviour are as follows: first, I encourage them to develop a flexible attitude towards the conditions that the person thinks they need before taking action (see Table 6.3). Second, I encourage them to take action in the absence of these conditions. Finally, I help them to respond to any DROs about doing either of these two things.

Tolerating discomfort

In both areas of self-control that I have discussed, it is important that the person is prepared to tolerate discomfort, see the reason for doing so and commit themself to doing so if they are going to sustain any changes that they may make.

Other emotional problems

While the previous categories identified discrete but general themes, the category that I am calling 'other emotional problems' is a catch-all one that contains a number of emotional problems. The problems in this category were discussed in 42 of the total number of 245 conversations (17.1%) (see Table 6.1). Of these 42 volunteers, 31 were women (73.8%) and 11 were men (26.2%). When we look a little more closely at this category (see Table 6.9), we find that guilt, hurt and shame were the three most commonly raised issues within this general category. Because of their similarity, I will discuss guilt and shame together.

Table 6.9 Themes raised by volunteers in the theme category: other emotional problems

Theme	Number
Guilt	13
Hurt	11
Shame	7
Jealousy	3
Problem with responsibility	3
Envy	2
OCD	2
Avoidance of negative feelings	1
Other emotional problems: total	**42**

Guilt and shame

Guilt (n = 13) and shame (n = 7) accounted for almost half of the issues (47.6%) raised by volunteers in the catch-all category of 'other emotional problems'.

Understanding guilt and shame

Guilt and shame are both similar and different in some respects. They are similar in that they both are underpinned by a rigid attitude and an extreme self-devaluation attitude. They are different in three major ways:

- **Different adversities at 'A'.**[5] When the person feels guilt at 'C', they tend to feel guilty about (a) violating their moral code, (b) failing to live up to their moral code and (c) harming someone and/or hurting someone's feelings. By contrast, when the person feels shame at 'C', they tend to feel ashamed about (a) falling very short of their ideal, (b) something highly negative being revealed about them (or about a group with whom they identify) by themself or by others and (c) others looking down on or shunning them (or a group with whom they identify). Remember, though, that it is the rigid and extreme attitudes about these 'A's that lead to guilt and shame, not the 'A's on their own.
- **Different content of self-devaluation attitudes at 'B'.** While self-devaluation attitudes underpin guilt and shame, the content of these self-devaluation attitudes is different. In guilt, they point to the moral worth of the person (e.g. "I'm bad, wicked or evil"), while in shame, they point to the social worth of the person (e.g. "I'm defective, disgusting or diminished").
- **Associated with different behaviours.** When a person experiences guilt, they tend to act in different ways than when they experience shame (see Appendix 1).

Dealing with guilt and shame

When helping volunteers with their guilt and shame problems, I tend to encourage them to:

- **Set a goal concerning their adversity at 'A'.** As discussed throughout this book, my approach to VBTCs is adversity-focused. This means that, whenever possible, I try to help the person deal effectively with their actual or inferred adversity at 'A'. Thus, I will often encourage them to assume temporarily that their 'A' is true. Having done so, I will help them set a healthy goal in the face of the assumed-to-be-true adversity. The healthy alternative to guilt is remorse,[6] which is based on a flexible and non-extreme USA attitude and associated with a number of behaviours outlined in Appendix 1. The healthy alternative to shame is disappointment,[7] which is again based on a flexible and non-extreme USA attitude and associated with a number of behaviours again outlined in Appendix 1. The issue of setting healthy negative emotions as goals does take some time and involves me identifying and responding to one or more DROs that the person has. If, after this, such DROs remain, I will help the person in the way that they nominate, which may mean bypassing dealing with the adversity at 'A.'

- **Develop a flexible attitude towards 'A'.** I tend to help the person accept their strong desire, but acknowledge that they don't have to meet their desire. Thus, with the person who has a shame problem, for example, I encourage them to see the following: that while there is nothing wrong with their strong desire not to fall very short of their high standards, the important point is that they acknowledge that they are not immune from doing so and neither do they have to have such immunity. Dealing with relevant DROs is an important part of doing this.

- **Develop a USA attitude towards 'A'.** Both guilt and shame involve self-devaluation as discussed above. Given this, it is important that I help the volunteer develop an appropriate non-extreme attitude of USA. I refer the reader to the 'Self-esteem problems' section above for a discussion of this issue.

- **Rehearse their new attitude in the session, if possible.** If there is time, I like to give the volunteer some experience in rehearsing their new developing attitude during our conversation. This helps them to get used to the idea that they can work towards a healthier attitude and it may also throw up one or more DROs that I need to discuss with them before our conversation draws to a close.

- **Plan to implement their flexible and/or USA attitudes in imagery and in real life.** Usually, a person with a guilt problem or a shame problem resonates more with the flexible attitude or the USA attitude that I have helped them to develop. Consequently, I usually feature that attitude in helping the person to plan how to implement it both in their mind's eye and in their everyday life.

Hurt

Hurt featured in 11 of the 42 conversations (26.2%) that I had with volunteers in the catch-all category of 'other emotional problems'.

Understanding hurt

When a volunteer brings a problem with hurt, I have the following points in my mind as I strive to help myself and the person understand their experience:

- **Does the person take responsibility for their feelings?** When a person feels hurt, it is usually about a situation where they think that another person with whom they are in a relationship is less invested in that relationship than they are or they think that another person has treated them unfairly in some way. Does the person take responsibility for their feelings (the 'B–C' model) or do they think that the other person's treatment of them makes them feel hurt?
- **Does the person see their hurt as problematic?** Even if the person does take responsibility for creating their hurt feelings, they may see their response to the other person's behaviour as being healthy and legitimate. In determining whether or not this is the case, I use the behavioural differences between hurt and sorrow (outlined in Appendix 1) to help me and the volunteer reach a consensus on this point.
- **Identifying 'A'.** Once the volunteer has agreed that their feelings of hurt are problematic, I will use Windy's Magic Question (see Chapter 5) to help us both find out what the person feels most hurt about.
- **Identifying 'B'.** There are two types of hurt: self-pity-based hurt and self-devaluation-based hurt. Both types share the same rigid attitude (e.g. "You must not treat me unfairly after all I have done for you"), but can be distinguished by the extreme attitudes that are derived from the rigid attitude. In self-pity-based hurt, there tends to be an awfulising attitude or a discomfort intolerance attitude (e.g. "You must not treat me unfairly after all I have done for you *and I can't bear it that you have. Poor me!*"). By contrast, in self-devaluation-based hurt, there will be a self-devaluation attitude (e.g. "You must not treat me unfairly after all I have done for you *and the fact that you have proves that I am unworthy*").

Dealing with hurt

In helping the volunteer deal with their problem with hurt, I have the following points in mind.

Set a goal concerning their adversity at 'A'. As with other unhealthy negative emotions, such as guilt and shame above, once the volunteer has acknowledged that their hurt feelings are problematic, I help them to set a goal concerning their adversity at 'A'. The healthy alternative to hurt is sorrow,[8] which is based on a flexible and non-extreme attitude and is associated with several behaviours again outlined in Appendix 1. I will once again identify and respond to any DROs to sorrow being a healthy alternative to hurt.

Help the person develop a flexible attitude

When a volunteer is experiencing hurt, I have found it important to acknowledge how they feel and validate their desire for better treatment from the other person. For them to accept the grim reality that the other person does not have to treat them better, it is important that I add what I call some 'sweeteners', since I am asking them to swallow a bitter pill. These sweeteners take the form of adverbs such as 'sadly' or 'regrettably', as in "I may want to be treated fairly by my boss, but regrettably, he doesn't have to do so" (see Chapter 12).

When dealing with self-pity-based hurt, help the person take the horror out of the badness and/or tolerate the discomfort

In self-pity-based hurt, the person says things like, "I feel hard done by," and, "It's so unfair." Their attitude towards themself needs to be understood in the context of a cruel world that allows such unfairness to happen to them when they do not deserve it. In addition to helping the person understand that, sadly, just because they don't deserve to be treated badly, it does not follow that they must not be so treated, I do one of two things: I either help them to take the horror out of this badness or to see that they can tolerate this adversity and that it's worth tolerating. Finally, I help them to see that they are not a poor person (as in 'poor me'), but a person who is in a poor situation.

When dealing with self-devaluation-based hurt, help the person develop a 'USA' attitude

In self-devaluation-based hurt, the person equates their worth with how the other treats them. It is as if they adhere to the equation 'bad treatment equals bad person'. In helping the person with this type of hurt, I encourage them not to equate their worth with how the other person behaves towards them and to personalise the alternative idea of 'it's bad, I'm not. I'm fallible'.

Help the person understand why others treat them badly

Although in a VBTC I only have the time to deal with one concrete example of the person's hurt problem, I try to ascertain if the person reports being treated badly or unfairly by others often. If so, then after I have helped them to deal with their hurt about the specific example, and if we have the time, I ask them to think about why they may encounter bad treatment from so many people. Here they may say things such as "It's because I'm too soft," in which case I ask them to identify the block to being firm with people and we do some work on dealing with this block if there is sufficient time.

When this issue is the prominent one in the conversation, after addressing the block, I help them to practise firmly asserting themself in a role play where I play the role of the other person who has treated them unfairly.

In this chapter, I have discussed how I tend to make sense of and respond to a plethora of issues raised by volunteers within the VBTC context. Let me reiterate a point I made at the beginning of the chapter: I also place much emphasis on the views that volunteers have of their issues and how they think these issues can best be tackled and I incorporate their ideas during our discussions whenever possible.

In the second part of this book, I will present and discuss several conversations I have had with volunteers who have given their written consent for me to include these with my commentary in this book.

Notes

1 Brazil, Greece, Israel, the Netherlands, Peru, Romania, Serbia, Slovenia and Turkey.
2 The personal domain is a kind of psychological space that contains anything that the individual deems to be personally valuable.

3 See also a training video on YouTube: https://contextualconsulting.co.uk/insights/passengers-on-the-bus-metaphor-acting-out-in-a-group.
4 For a fuller discussion of these points and others, see Dryden (1999) and Ellis (2005).
5 Throughout this section, I will make use of the 'Situational ABC' framework that I introduced and discussed in Chapter 3.
6 The term 'remorse' is my suggested term for the healthy alternative to guilt. In practice, I will use the volunteer's own language.
7 The term 'disappointment' is, again, my suggested term for the healthy alternative to shame. In practice, I will use the volunteer's own language.
8 The term 'sorrow' is, once again, my suggested term for the healthy alternative to hurt. In practice, I will, as before, use the volunteer's own language.

Part 2

Conversations

Chapter 7

"I need to know that a large, angry man won't attack me": Lauren

Length of conversation = 27 minutes and 6 seconds

Lauren attended a one-day workshop that I gave on REBT in Brighton organised by the Brighton Person-Centred Community on 14 June 2008 at which I conducted three live therapy demonstrations sessions.

WINDY: OK, Lauren, which particular issue would you like to discuss with me today?

LAUREN: You mentioned something current and I would say this is a recurring process for me. I'm a transgender person and I transitioned quite a few years ago now, but I do find that I still experience a certain amount of fear about that issue. In a sense, I'm exposing myself here, but, obviously, this is a relatively safe environment, I think. But I do find that fear is still a problem for me at times, the fear of being exposed in an inappropriate place. And I feel that that fear is disproportionate to reality.

WINDY: And how do you feel about being afraid?

[Here I was checking to see if Lauren had a meta-emotional problem, in this case about her fear. As is clear below, she does, but she chose to target the original fear problem.]

LAUREN: That's a good question. Frustrated.

WINDY: Frustrated with?

LAUREN: With the fact that I'm still afraid. Having been through all sorts of therapy for the gender transition process itself, which is a bit of a minefield, really, of psychiatrists and doctors, and all the rest of it. It feels like there's an immovable object, at times.

WINDY: Maybe we can look at a specific example of your fear, something that may lend itself in order for us to put into practice anything we talk about today. Can you give me a specific example of your fear?

[I very quickly ask Lauren for a specific example of her fear problem.]

LAUREN: I can, actually, and it's interesting, because I think it's something that could impinge on my practice. I'm a relatively new counsellor. I had a client, obviously respecting all confidence here, who was male and quite angry. I don't think it really impinged on the session too much, but I did feel afterwards that, at the back of my mind was this fear, that if this person sees me as a transgendered woman as opposed to just a woman, there could be a problem. That's an example of when I feel it's inappropriate. It's one thing to be scared if somebody's threatening you in a pub or something like that, that feels almost like a rational fear, if you like, but this felt rather irrational to me.

WINDY: Well, let's suppose it is irrational just for the moment, how do you feel about being irrational in this sense?

LAUREN: I guess I don't like being irrational. You're hitting the nail on the head there.

WINDY: What's the feeling?

LAUREN: Nervous, very nervous.

WINDY: About being irrational?

LAUREN: I think it's anger, actually.

WINDY: Anger at?

LAUREN: I'm angry with myself.

WINDY: For being irrational?

LAUREN: For not being able to rationalise away the fear.

WINDY: So, I'm hearing there are two components of this: one is the idea that you are afraid, and we'll look at that, and you're afraid of what might happen if a person like the person you're working with discovers that you are a transgendered person. The other aspect is, when you observe that you're not being rational, you feel angry with yourself. As you reflect on that now, which, do you think, is the most problematic aspect of that?

LAUREN: I think the fear of the consequences. The first part about what might happen. As I talk about it now it feels like that's probably what's driving the process, having had some bad experiences in the past.

WINDY: OK. Well, let's focus on that and, if we need to, we can come back and do some work on your anger with yourself for not handling this irrational issue. Just before we do that work, I'm wondering what, for you, would be a successful outcome in dealing with this particular issue.

[I ask quite quickly for Lauren's goal.]

LAUREN: I suppose, to feel appropriate fear if and when I'm threatened and for that fear to do what I think fear is meant to do, which is this fight or flight. If I'm in a threatening situation, which is very rare, then perhaps fear would be appropriate and it's a signal. Other than that, I'd like to see the back of it, really. That would be a very successful outcome.

WINDY: And by seeing the back of it you mean what?

LAUREN: Not to feel afraid.

WINDY: If I understand this, when you say "not to feel afraid," do you mean like in the situation with your clients, that you won't think that he might discover that you're a transgendered person or that he might do so, but that you wouldn't react with fear?

LAUREN: As you're dismantling it a bit, which is good, I'm starting to see the separate elements in it. I think it has a lot to do with my thinking, which I think is what you were driving at there. I think the part that I don't like is the physical part.

WINDY: The physical part?

LAUREN: Yes. The physical nervousness, the sense of being off balance. I do cope with having that thought that that fear is a possibility. The cycle I would want to break is the way it triggers me into an almost physical reaction, which can almost feel self-fulfilling, in a way.

WINDY: So, in a way, the problem for you, as we look at this and dismantle it, is not so much the thinking, because, I suppose, there is always a possibility that a person may actually find out about you and actually cause a problem for you, but it's your feeling response about that, that is the problem.

[As Lauren notes, I am attempting to dismantle her problem so I can understand it better.]

LAUREN: Yes.

WINDY: How would you put that into your own words, in terms of the response?

LAUREN: Feeling a wobbly tummy, shaky, kind of wanting to run away, if you take it to the extreme.

WINDY: What, for you, would be a healthy response if the worst happened, if he discovers that you're a transgendered person and, maybe, causes a problem for you?

LAUREN: The strange thing is, quite often my response, when that does happen, the situation is generally less bad than I think it's going to be. In fact, it can be quite positive at times.

WINDY: So, let's see if we can find out the scenario you have in your mind rather than the reality you actually encounter. With this new client, what are you afraid of? What is the scenario in your head that you're particularly afraid of?

[Sometimes when people discover that what they fear dos not happen, it changes their inferences at 'A'. Thus, they no longer anticipate the threat. However, at other times, discovering that the feared outcome does not happen does not change the person's inference at 'A'. This seems to be the case with Lauren and is why I make it clear that we should address the feared scenario in her mind rather than the reality that she encounters.]

LAUREN: A large, angry man attacking me.

WINDY: And how might this large, angry man attack you? Verbally? Physically?

LAUREN: Physically. Verbalising, I can take, really. I've been in quite a lot of therapy and I can trace a lot of that to events and things in my childhood, but there's still this sense that it doesn't quite shift. The knowing is not quite enough.

WINDY: The knowing about what?

LAUREN: The rational says, "I have this fear because I have been attacked in the past by large, angry men." So, OK, I can see the connection, but this is still happening for me. Sometimes it feels, as I said, inappropriate and annoying, actually. That's the anger part.

WINDY: Let me just share with you a hypothesis and we can either accept it or kick it out. Is this man large and angry?

[I meant is the client to whom she was referring large and angry. However, she seemed to know what I meant.]

LAUREN: Yes, he's six foot two and has got anger issues.

WINDY: I guess there is a possibility that he might attack you, but if we were to give you one ingredient in a situation that would get rid of your fear at that point, what would it be? So, you're working with him, he's large and angry and we can't make him small and placid, what one ingredient would take the anxiety away?

[Here I am using Windy's Magic Question to identify Lauren's 'A' (see Chapter 5).]

LAUREN: On the fantasy level?

WINDY: Yes.

LAUREN: To know that there's absolutely no possibility that he could ever know my history.

[This is Lauren's 'A'.]

WINDY: And if we can't give you that absolute guarantee?

LAUREN: I do have a panic button, which, obviously, I would use.

WINDY: You've got two panic buttons, it sounds like – an internal one and an external one. If I can't give you that guarantee, what?

LAUREN: No, I'm looking for a guarantee.

WINDY: OK, let me just go over a couple of possible attitudes that might be in there, because, from where I'm coming from, either you're thinking, at the time when you're really anxious, "I'd like to have a guarantee that this guy's not going to attack me, but it really is not necessary. I still don't like the uncertainty, but it's not terrible," or, "No, no, no, I've got to know for absolute certain that this guy isn't going to attack me."

[In using my WRAP method (see Chapter 5), I make an error and use the 'A' Lauren previously gave me (i.e. "not knowing whether this man will attack me") rather than what she just said (i.e. "not having a guarantee that this man does not know my history").]

LAUREN: Yes. I mean, I can see that's completely unrealistic, now that you've said that.

WINDY: Which one do you think you're operating on when you get anxious in this situation – the idea you'd like it or at that time you really do need it?

LAUREN: I'm probably operating more from the desire for guarantee.

WINDY: Just the desire or the need? Because the desire is saying, "I want the guarantee, but I don't need it," and the need is saying, "No, I have to know for sure."

LAUREN: I can't help coming from person-centred here, but in configurations of self, there's a part of me that absolutely wants a guarantee.

[Lauren is a recently qualified person-centred counsellor and is putting this in her own frame. I am happy to go along with this frame.]

WINDY: Yes, that's right. You see, what happens there is that, when you don't get the guarantee, then because that is so important, so crucial, you almost invent a scenario which goes along with that, i.e. being attacked. Whereas, if you were really to operate from a part of you which said, "I really do like one but I don't need one," then there's still that possibility, but how likely is it in your mind?

[I am explaining to Lauren that her unmet need for a guarantee that she won't be attacked leads to her creating mental scenarios where she is attacked. I explained this in greater detail in Chapter 6.]

LAUREN: Yes, and that feels more adult as well.

WINDY: So, my hypothesis is that, in that situation you're not just saying, "I'd really like to know, but it really is not necessary and, if it happens, well, it's probably not going to be as bad as I think it is. I've got this panic button here," it's, "No, I have to have it and, if I don't have it, horrible things are going to happen and I'll be attacked."

LAUREN: Actually, in a sense that's even more true outside of that situation. I picked the thing with the client because it's just at the front of my mind, but if I think of the ways I experience the fear out in the world, as it were, yes, I think it's usually when I'm looking for some sort of guarantee, and something can trigger it.

[Lauren generalises from this specific situation. I then go back to the situation, but I wish that I had acknowledged this 'specific to general' connection as it could have proved useful to have done so later.]

WINDY: In the therapy situation, when you're feeling anxious like that, are you doing anything in the situation to try and reassure yourself that this isn't going to happen?

[I am checking whether Lauren uses any safety-seeking strategies in situ.]

LAUREN: Probably not really, in the sense I'm very focused on the client, or I'm trying to be very focused on the client, and I am. I feel I am present. And that's one of the things that frustrates me, actually, as a person relatively new to therapy, is anything which I think makes me less present, I'd rather get rid of that or, at least, get some kind of handle on it.

WINDY: OK, you're having the next session with this chap. You start to get anxious. Could you imagine really going to the root of this and saying, "This is about my absolutely wanting a guarantee"? What do you think you need to remind yourself at that particular point, to be healthily concerned about the prospect, but not anxious about it and over-estimating?

LAUREN: Well, I think you just said it, really – be healthily concerned about the prospect. I'm working with a client who may be prone to outbursts of anger, not necessarily at me, and, actually, I experience a lot of empathy with this person. I like him, so it feels very out of context. I'm very aware of it being my stuff. If I was being wholly congruent you might say I should share it with the client, but that doesn't really feel appropriate. That would be like it was about me.

WINDY: So, that's the other thing, you could really go in there saying, "Obviously, I'd like to know that this is not going to happen, but I don't need the guarantee."

[In the above two exchanges, Lauren emphasises the affective part of the message and I emphasise the attitudinal part. This may reflect our different therapeutic orientations.]

LAUREN: I like that, yes.

WINDY: Let me just come back to the other thing, because you were saying you get angry with yourself for having this fear, and one or two other times, when you were talking, it's almost like you want to eliminate from you aspects of you that you don't particularly...

LAUREN: It's a bit all or nothing.

WINDY: Right, yes. I'm just wondering if we can do a little bit of work on that and look at what you're angry with yourself for being as afraid as you are. What are you particularly angry about with yourself for being, let's say, inappropriately afraid in this situation?

[Having come to some kind of resolution on the fear issue, I invite Lauren to do some work on her meta-emotional problem.]

LAUREN: It feels like it probably taps into my anger at finding myself having to deal with this particular situation in my life, anyway. I mean, you don't plan to be born this way, or I don't or did. So, there's that anger there, at being transgendered. I have worked through a lot of that, so that's relevant with the anger. But I'm just wondering, I'm thinking out loud now, if it's an offshoot of that, being angry that the consequences are this, that and the other, that sometimes I have to, perhaps, be a little bit more vigilant.

WINDY: A kind of 'not fair' aspect of anger?

LAUREN: Yes, it's not fair.

WINDY: How would you put that into your own words?

LAUREN: It's not fucking fair.

WINDY: And how would you like to deal with that fairness that acknowledges the fact that this is a strong desire of yours, but without that anger?

LAUREN: I think, in some sort of strange way, sitting here talking with you now is bringing it right into the present moment, is part of me working through that fear, possibly, and exposing myself to something manageable. I mean, although I'm coming from a humanistic place, I am aware of some of the ideas of REBT and I did find it really interesting, which is why I'm here. 'It's not fair' went right in. That hit me at an emotional level. I would see that as the root, in some ways, of where this feeling comes from in my past. It's not fair – the number of times I said that as a kid.

[Note the emotional resonance that Lauren displays with the unfair-ness issue.]

WINDY: When you think about it, just to bring it back into the concept we're talking about with this client, for me, 'it's not fair' is almost like the tip of the iceberg. I'm not quite sure whether you mean, "It's not fair that the world has dumped this on me when I don't deserve it," or the idea that, "I'm doing this to myself and I'm not being fair to myself." Just look at that particular situation at the moment and then we can look at it more broadly. When you think it's not fair that you're anxious, in the sense that you are with this chap, what's the aspect of fairness?

[While Lauren speaks of the 'unfairness' issue as a general one, I am applying it to the situation in which she experienced it with her client.]

LAUREN: Like you said, that's the tip of the iceberg. It's interesting because I feel guilt coming in, actually, as I'm saying this, but I'll go with it anyway – it feels not fair that I have this extra burden, which sounds like a real cross on the back, but it feels like an extra thing. As I'm saying that, I'm thinking, am I just doing this to myself?

WINDY: Who are you angry about? To me, anger needs an object: either the self, the world or some other person. When you say about you being given an extra burden.

[To facilitate the assessment of this meta-problem, I ask Lauren for the object of her anger.]

LAUREN: God, and I'm not particularly a religious person. I'm generally not angry at other people. I'm generally quite good at accepting people as human beings, but I'm not so good at accepting it in myself.

WINDY: And what is that extra burden?

LAUREN: Being transgendered. It makes me cringe to say that.

WINDY: In what way?

LAUREN: It feels like such a martyr trip – oh, poor me! But, here I am. I feel it's right to just open that out. In a way, it feels quite good to sit here and actually hand it over to you and hear your hypothesis and somebody saying, "How about this?" and, "How about that?"

WINDY: Let's go with the idea that it is an extra burden.

LAUREN: Lots of things are, though.

WINDY: I'm hearing that you're giving yourself two burdens for the price of one, because you're not only saying, "This is an extra burden," you're also saying, "But I shouldn't have this extra burden."

[I am using REBT theory here to guide my hypothesis:

A = I have an extra burden.
B = I shouldn't have this extra burden.
C = Anger.]

LAUREN: You're right.

WINDY: Why shouldn't you have this extra burden?

LAUREN: Why me, why not me? Yes. I don't have any answer for you.

WINDY: We can give great ideas why it would be great not to have that extra burden, couldn't we?

LAUREN: Yes.

WINDY: Anyway, that's something for you to think about.

LAUREN: It's helpful, actually. In a way, it might be anathema to some person-centred people, but to dissect it a bit and look at the ingredients is quite helpful.

WINDY: Well, the way I would put it within a person-centred framework is actually doing what Truax and Carkhuff called 'specificity' – I'm being very specific with you.

LAUREN: What's just dropped into my mind as well is, this client I was talking about, I feel, instinctively, he's wanting more than a purely person-centred approach, is wanting to look at anger in terms of triggers. I'm not sure I have the skills to do that, but that remains to be seen.

WINDY: How would you summarise the work that we've done today, if you were to step back and reflect on it?

LAUREN: I'd say it's helpful.

WINDY: In terms of the content, first of all.

LAUREN: I feel like I've brought my fear to you. In person-centred theoretical terms it felt like I'm voluntarily externalising my locus of evaluation, but I'm doing it consensually, in a way, and saying, "There you go." I really do feel like you're looking at it from my point of view and you're trying to get inside my frame of reference, which is what you said.

WINDY: In terms of my frame of reference, if I can share that, that, in a way, what we've been doing is looking that, underneath this fear you've got with this man is this need that you have for a guarantee that it isn't going to happen, that you've got to know this isn't going to happen. Because you can't convince yourself that it isn't going to happen, that leads you to overestimate it happening.

LAUREN: There's a key phrase you used there, because I can't convince myself. That's it! And because I have any number of scenarios as a kid, I can draw on worst-case scenarios. I think you would probably call that 'awfulising'.

WINDY: Yes. The other aspect is looking at your attitude towards your responses. I thought you were going to go more into the anger at yourself for being inappropriately afraid, but you got more into anger at God because he's given you a burden, and he shouldn't do that.

LAUREN: Yes, it feels that that's probably the wider picture. The specific anger is drawing on that pool of anger, which is there to be drawn on.

[Lauren and I are sharing our own perspectives in the summary, but with reference to one another's theoretical perspectives.]

WINDY: Is there anything you think you might put into practice?

LAUREN: I think an awareness of what I'm actually doing, in terms of my thought processes. I think that's something I can certainly use, especially the thing about guarantees. That's what I would take: the guarantees and the fact that I can't convince myself that the worst is not going to happen. It is upside down in a view of feelings that I'm used to, but I feel quite open to it, that I might be creating the feeling in myself, to some extent.

[This is the 'one thing' that Lauren is going to take away with her (Keller & Papasan, 2012).]

WINDY: Although we've been looking at a specific example, what you could do is then say, "OK, if ever I'm anxious about an event, then I'm going to question myself whether I'm actually demanding a guarantee about the situation." You can generalise it to other situations.

LAUREN: Yes, thank you.

Follow-up

Nine years and three months after the conversation with Lauren, she sent me the following to be used in this book:

It's very interesting to look back at this session with Windy from the perspective I have now, several years on. At the time of the seminar I didn't know that much about REBT. I think I probably saw it as a sort of 'posh' version of CBT, which I also probably didn't know that much about! My own training had been in a Rogerian/Humanistic person-centred model, although my

Diploma course did certainly include a certain amount of integrative content, and I was always interested in other models, having experienced personal therapy with practitioners from other modalities. Thus, my attendance at Windy's seminar.

Looking at the transcript of the session, I'm struck by how, as soon as I spoke about my fear, Windy immediately asked me how I felt *about* being afraid, thus bringing the focus very quickly to what I now understand as 'meta disturbance', i.e. feelings *about* feelings. I can see a contrast here with a strict Rogerian approach which might have been to simply reflect back to me the fact that I felt fearful in the situation I had described. We could probably have spent an entire session exploring the quality of that fear, in a more Rogerian way, but it's debatable as to how helpful that would have been. By Windy 'cutting to the chase' in the way he did we were able to 'zoom in' to the key components of the issue very promptly, e.g. not just my fear, but my frustration with myself for *being* fearful, and to home in on some of the unspoken beliefs and demands which were contributing to my sense of emotional disturbance.

The next striking aspect of the transcript is how quickly Windy moved to asking for a *specific* instance of the fear. This was very helpful. I think by being specific, the session again moved forward and became more focused, rather than, for instance, dissipating into an exploration of numerous different situations in which I felt this type of fear – I could probably have come up with quite a few. A purely non-directive approach would almost certainly not have got this far, this soon.

As the session progressed two areas of disturbance emerged, Windy was able to spot this, summarise the components, and invite me to choose where we would focus. Again, specificity. From this point on, reading the transcript, it's striking how quickly Windy is forming a hypothesis (which he puts to me) about my unspoken *demand* for a guarantee that I'm absolutely not going to be attacked in any way, and also my catastrophising around what the ensuing scenario is likely to look like. In regards to the situation I was describing, I was able to get a sense quite quickly of how I was thinking: "I absolutely *must* have a guarantee that x will not happen. And if x does happen it's going to be absolutely *terrible*." It all seems a bit obvious in hindsight, but it wasn't prior to this session. I can also see how Windy began to introduce the idea of *goals*, asking me what a realistic and successful outcome would be for me, while bringing into the open and questioning my totalising demand for an absolute guarantee.

Looking back, I think the session with Windy helped me not only with the specific situation we discussed, but also to get a better handle on the way thinking can affect feeling. I think this is one of the great strengths of REBT, the transferable nature of the cognitive skills which one can learn with this approach. Prior to encountering REBT, I did tend to prioritise or even somewhat deify emotions, to see feeling as somehow inherently truthful and trustworthy *in of itself*. Working with Windy and gaining a little more understanding of the interactive, symbiotic relationship between thought and feeling undoubtedly shifted my perspective and with hindsight, this short session was perhaps something of a turning point in that process of understanding.

I'd add that, as someone trained in a model where the Rogerian 'Core Conditions' were considered crucial and at the very least 'necessary', I found Windy's presence and approach wholly consistent with those conditions, i.e. I experienced him as empathic, congruent and expressing unconditional positive regard towards me throughout the encounter. There has been considerable debate in the field as to whether the Core Conditions are 'necessary *and* sufficient' or necessary but not necessarily sufficient. I think it can be readily seen that, in this session at least, there was a great deal more going on than *only* the Core Conditions, and that the session's 'success' hinged on a number of key *directive* interventions by Windy which quickly built a kind of 'therapeutic infrastructure', albeit anchored on the foundations which the Core Conditions undoubtedly provide.

As a therapeutic experience this session was certainly sufficient for me, as a relatively inexperienced counsellor, to arouse a greater interest in cognitive approaches, REBT in particular, and to gain a great deal of respect for the modality. This respect, to be honest, is something I've not always experienced within Person Centred/Humanistic circles, where some practitioners seem to be somewhat dismissive or even hostile towards CBT, REBT or pluralistic ways of working. This may be partly political, perhaps there is a certain amount of resentment at the success such approaches have had within the NHS, but also I think there may be an assumption for some practitioners that cognitive modalities only 'scratch the surface' of the problem, an assumption perhaps shared by some psychodynamic folk too.

I believe that assumption to be wrong, in the sense that, no matter how we may conceptualise the human psyche, the entirety of a person is *always* present in the room. How could it be otherwise? Speaking personally I have experienced psychodynamic 'deep' approaches as a client, and I'm certainly aware of the 'deeper' aspects of my own fear, including some of the prototypical childhood experiences around which it originally constellated. However, simply 'ventilating the pain' is in my view sometimes unhelpful, and if therapy is in the business of offering practical help to people – and I think and hope that it is – Windy certainly demonstrated for me in this session some very pragmatic and accessible ways in which I could work with and manage both my fear and my thoughts and feelings *about* my fear, and in this respect what I learned has proved to be invaluable. So thank you very much Windy for helping me to both 'right size' my fear and to gain a deeper insight into how my thinking around my fear can affect both my behaviour and my sense of inner emotional equilibrium.

Chapter 8

Understanding how the OCD mind works and acting constructively: Brianna

Length of conversation = 21 minutes and 10 seconds

Brianna is a helping professional who attended a one-day workshop that I gave in Stratford-upon-Avon on 22 February 2013. She volunteered, seeking help for an OCD problem, and was prepared to discuss this in front of an audience of her peers. Later she gave me permission to include our interview in this book with commentary and provided a short email follow-up report four years and four months after the conversation, which appears at the end of the chapter.

WINDY: OK, do you want to give me your first name?

BRIANNA: I'm Brianna.

WINDY: OK, Brianna, what problem would you like to discuss with me today?

BRIANNA: Well, I have a history of OCD and a vast range of OCD behaviours, which are mostly under control, but there's one particular situation that I would like to stop, because it gets in the way of my life. Others I'm quite happy with.

WINDY: 'You're quite happy with' meaning?

BRIANNA: Some of them I quite like.

WINDY: You quite like?

BRIANNA: They're my little quirks.

WINDY: OK. But this particular behaviour you don't quite like and you would rather not act in the way that you do. Is that correct?

BRIANNA: Yes, I've done it for a long time.

WINDY: OK. Could you be a little bit more specific about what that is?

BRIANNA: It's a repetitive behaviour, actually, now I'm talking about it, it's so stupid and I know it's stupid, but I check my en suite bathroom repeatedly, but only if I've actually been into the bathroom. So, if I don't use the bathroom, that particular room, all day, I don't have a compulsion to go and check it.

WINDY: Right, OK.

BRIANNA: But once I've been in it I have to check it in a certain way before I leave.

WINDY: And what is that way?

BRIANNA: It does sound so stupid now I'm saying it out loud, I have to look behind the shower curtain, at the taps and at the shower head and then I have to look at the taps in the sink, and there's a bidet so I look at the taps there and the plugholes, and then I have a look at the toilet and the toilet roll, and then I have to do a visual sweep of the room and then I can leave.

WINDY: OK. Now, I noticed a couple of times that you said that, as we were talking, it was stupid.

[What I am thinking here is, "Does Brianna have a meta-problem – an emotional problem about her checking behaviour – and if so, is it going to interfere with the conversation I plan to have with her about her nominated problem?" I thus check this out with her.]

BRIANNA: Well, I know it's stupid, but I don't usually tell people about it.

WINDY: OK. How do you feel about having the problem?

BRIANNA: It's ridiculous. Well, I can justify it but it's ridiculous.

WINDY: And what's the emotion that goes along with that, 'it's ridiculous'?

BRIANNA: Well, embarrassment, I suppose.

WINDY: Is that sense of embarrassment going to stop us from talking about it today or not?

BRIANNA: No, I don't think so. I think I'm just aware that there's a room of people probably thinking, "That's completely nuts!" And I would agree with them, if that's what they thought.

[Brianna confirms that she does not have a meta-problem and her sense of embarrassment will not interfere with the conversation on her checking behaviour.]

WINDY: OK. We'll do a poll later on that. Of course, being counsellors, none of them will think you're *completely* nuts. So, now, do you do this behaviour in a particular order?

BRIANNA: Yes.

WINDY: And it has to be in that order?

BRIANNA: Yes.

WINDY: And if you don't do it in that order what happens?

BRIANNA: If I try to cut into the order or just talk myself into it being perfectly OK without me doing it, I get a shadowy feeling.

WINDY: A shadowy feeling?

BRIANNA: Yes, that something out of my visual field will have done something.

WINDY: Something out of your visual field would've done something?

BRIANNA: Well, if I just look at that side of the room and not over there, there might be something there that I haven't noticed.

WINDY: Like what?

BRIANNA: Like somebody hiding behind the shower curtains, like a *Psycho* kind of scenario.

WINDY: Right, OK. Now, do you do this behaviour if you go into the bathroom or only if you do certain activities in the bathroom, to help me to understand that?

BRIANNA: I don't do it as I go in.

WINDY: Right. I mean, let's suppose you just went into the bathroom and...

BRIANNA: Oh yeah, if I haven't gone to have a shower or gone to the loo or anything, if I've just gone in to change a toilet roll or gone in to change a hand towel, I will do it before I leave the room.

WINDY: Right, OK. So, it's if you go into the bathroom to change a toilet roll or to just clean your hands, you're still doing the behaviour.

BRIANNA: Yes.

WINDY: You will? OK. And how about when you're in the shower?

BRIANNA: Oh, that's fine. If I'm in the shower I'm just showering, I'm not checking anything. I can't leave the room without doing it.

WINDY: 'Can't' meaning physically unable to or 'can't' meaning it's very difficult to?

BRIANNA: Actually it's quite easy to leave the room, but I know I will have to come back and still do it.

WINDY: Let's suppose I suggested, in terms of imagination, that you went into the bathroom, had a shower or whatever and then came out without doing the rituals, how would you feel so that you would believe that you would have to go back and do the rituals?

[What I am doing here is trying to identify an emotion that she would experience if she did not do her rituals, an emotion that would result in her going back to do them. I am looking for the 'emotional C' here.]

BRIANNA: I get to a particular point on the stairs where I have to turn round and go back.

WINDY: OK. Now, let's focus on that particular point on the stairs, what's going on at that particular point on the stairs?

BRIANNA: A sort of internal debate which is, "Don't be silly, it'll be fine," as opposed to something that doesn't have words attached to it, but is a kind of knotted general anxiety feeling.

WINDY: And that's what you call your 'shadowy' feeling, is it?

BRIANNA: No, the shadowy thing is if I'm in the room and not checking properly.

WINDY: Right, if you're not checking properly. So, a shadowy feeling is what you get when you're not checking properly, the knotted feeling in the stomach is what you'd get if you were to leave the room without checking.

BRIANNA: The shadowy feeling is because I have to sweep the entire room. It's when I'm checking the things, I have to include the entire room so no bit is gone unchecked.

WINDY: So what's your goal here?

BRIANNA: I would like to not do this because it wastes my time.

WINDY: And feel what?

BRIANNA: And feel, I suppose, calm, OK about it.

WINDY: Well, maybe I can help you to do that over the long haul, but, initially, I don't think I'm going to be able to help you to do that. There are two things: one is when you're in the room to not do the rituals and you're still going to have that sense of discomfort, though, aren't you?

BRIANNA: On the stairs.

WINDY: Or actually in the room, if you don't do it. Let's suppose you don't do it. So, the shadowy feeling only happens when you're not doing it in the right order.

BRIANNA: Yes.

WINDY: OK. So, on the stairs you're still going to have that knotted feeling.

BRIANNA: Mmm.

WINDY: Now, it's your relationship with that knotted feeling that we need to have a look at. What do you think your relationship is with that knotted feeling that would lead you to feel that you had to go back?

[Here, I am focusing on Brianna's 'knotted' sense of discomfort anxiety and offering her the perspective that it is her relationship with that feeling that leads to her rituals.]

BRIANNA: I'm not sure I understand what you mean.

WINDY: Well, I mean is it a pleasant feeling or an unpleasant feeling?

BRIANNA: No, it's unpleasant.

WINDY: Is it tolerable or intolerable?

BRIANNA: It's tolerable because I can, on occasion, get through it, but it's doubt.

WINDY: Doubt about what?

BRIANNA: Doubt that I have checked everything properly.

WINDY: Yes, but if you were to leave without checking at all how would you feel?

BRIANNA: Then it would be doubt about safety.

[Since Brianna's goal is to leave the bathroom without checking I focus on doubt-related anxiety about safety. Note that Brianna soon changes this to doubt about herself.]

WINDY: OK. So, the doubt would be safety. So, it's your relationship with that, then, we'll have to look at.

BRIANNA: I think so.

WINDY: Now, we don't need any prizes, because I'm not going to win the Nobel Prize for Counselling by saying this, but we know that you prefer not to have doubt. Is that correct?

BRIANNA: It's doubting myself, I think. I don't do doubt myself.

WINDY: OK, you'd rather not have that.

BRIANNA: Mmm.

WINDY: Could you help me to understand, then, whether you then go on to say, "Well, I prefer not to have this sense of doubting myself, but I don't have to be free of it, or I do have to be free of it." What leads you to go back to the room? The idea that you have to be free of it or that you don't have to be free of it?

BRIANNA: I guess that I do have to be free of it.

[Here, I am employing the 'WRAP' that I discussed in Chapter 5. Brianna's preference about not doubting herself is common to both her rigid attitude (i.e. "I prefer not to have this sense of doubting myself and therefore I must be free of it") and her flexible attitude (i.e. "I prefer not to have this sense of doubting myself, but I don't have to be free of it").]

WINDY: Now, as long as you believe that you have to be free of the doubt, you're going to go back.

BRIANNA: Well, I'd like to not feel that sick feeling.

WINDY: Right, but what I'm suggesting to you is that you may have to have that sick feeling for a while. I mean, when you overcame your OCD in other areas did you immediately not have the sick feeling or the anxiety feeling?

BRIANNA: No.

WINDY: So the same thing is likely to be the case here, isn't it? So then the question is, what's the alternative? It seems to me you have a choice, because we know that you would prefer not to have that sense of doubting yourself, but the choices are to believe that, "I don't have to be free of it," or, "I have to be free of it." Now, which idea is going to be more helpful to you?

BRIANNA: The thing that bothers me is if I can get to the point where I can say, "Well, it doesn't matter."

[When I begin to examine Brianna's rigid and flexible attitudes, she immediately responds by indicating that her goal is 'indifference', a goal that will lead to failure if pursued.]

WINDY: Which is what I'm actually not suggesting, because the idea of 'I'd prefer to be free of doubt' means that when you are in a state of doubt it's unpreferable, it's undesirable, it's unpleasant.

[I respond by clarifying that I am not advocating working towards indifference, which is not possible given that she has a preference not to doubt herself.]

BRIANNA: So, you're asking me to be able to get downstairs and still doubt and be OK with that?

WINDY: Not OK, I want you to feel un-OK with it because you're in an unpreferable state. See, you want to feel OK and I don't think I can do that. I don't think anybody can do that. You can do that. You know how you'd do that?

[Clarifying language is a common feature of my VBTC work. Here, Brianna thinks I am advocating 'being OK' with doubt. As I show in my response, she needs to feel 'un-OK' and that it is her goal to feel OK that would lead her back to using her rituals, which are designed to get rid of doubt. Brianna needs to stay with doubt, be 'un-OK' with it and tolerate this state while not using her rituals. I clarify this in the exchanges that follow.]

BRIANNA: Well, I'd probably go and use another OCD behaviour.

WINDY: Or you'd go back and do this sort of behaviour, because you're already saying, basically, "I've got to get rid of this feeling of doubt, I've got to get rid of this feeling of discomfort as quickly as possible," and the best way you've got to do that is either crack cocaine or your rituals, it seems to me.

BRIANNA: So, I can get downstairs and still feel, then what I do is distraction techniques. I think then I distract myself.

WINDY: Well, I think before you do that I think you need to practise the philosophy which is...

BRIANNA: Being doubtful.

WINDY: Well, and that it's unpreferable, but you don't have to get rid of it. You can proceed with doubt. And so, for example, let's take a situation where you would do the ritual then you go downstairs, what would you be doing after you go downstairs?

[Brianna discloses that she has gotten by in the past by using a range of distraction techniques. However, I am advocating that she focuses on her doubt (her adversity at 'A') and practise her flexible attitude (at 'B') without distracting herself. I then stress that she can do the very things she would do, but with doubt.]

BRIANNA: Get ready to go out or do some work or something.

WINDY: Well, you'd do exactly the same thing, right, but you'd do it with doubt. Right? Now, the other thing is if you're doing it with doubt you also need to have a different relationship to the thoughts, because let's suppose you do go downstairs, you haven't checked and you're living with the feeling of discomfort associated with the doubt, what would you be thinking at that point?

BRIANNA: That the bathroom will flood.

WINDY: OK. Now, what were you going to do about that thought?

BRIANNA: What, if I'm just trying to live with the doubt?

WINDY: Yep.

BRIANNA: I would think, well, how likely is it?
WINDY: No.
BRIANNA: Oh, OK.

[Brianna uses a seemingly rational response to her thought 'the bathroom will flood'. However, her response is meant to get rid of doubt-related anxiety and instead I suggest that she views such thoughts as part of the 'OCD' experience and understand it as such. In this approach, the person allows the thought to be rather than engaging with it, as my subsequent interventions clarify.]

WINDY: I'll tell you why: because that would be engaging with it.
BRIANNA: OK.
WINDY: You see? My suggestion is you need to say, "That's an OCD thought. I'm doing nothing about it. I'm going to let it be."
BRIANNA: So, I don't actually rationalise it.
WINDY: No. You recognise that it's part of the OCD experience and will fade away, with all probability, if you get on with whatever you're doing.
BRIANNA: Oh, OK.
WINDY: If you engage with it and say, "How likely is it?" then this other part of you will say, "Well, you never know." You know? And before you know it you're up there checking.
BRIANNA: That's exactly what I do.
WINDY: Exactly!
BRIANNA: Just on the off chance.
WINDY: Exactly, because, again, you're going to get the same. So, what I'm saying is, if you engage with either the thinking associated as opposed to saying, "OK, that's an OCD thought, I'm just going to go about my business. I'm not going to engage with it, I'm not going to try and get rid of it." The problem with distraction is you're trying to get rid of something as opposed to allowing it to fade away. So, let's just go over that and see what you think about this: you go into the bathroom, you do whatever it is, you come out, you start to feel that knotted feeling associated with doubt. You remind yourself, "OK, I'm in a state of doubt, I don't have to get rid of it, I don't like it, but I'm just going to go downstairs with it," and, "Oh yeah, that's the thought about, no, I'm not going to engage with that, I'm just going to go down, I'm going to get on with it." And that's going to be still going on in the background, but you are going to be

guided by your healthy mind not by your unhealthy OCD mind. Now, could you imagine doing that?

BRIANNA: I can imagine doing it, but I can also imagine another little voice in my head going, "Yeah, but that's you just pretending to have a healthy thought."

WINDY: OK. Now, is that part of the OCD experience?

BRIANNA: Yes, I guess so.

WINDY: So, all those thoughts you've got to recognise as OCD thoughts and not to be engaged with. It's not just the bathroom's going to flood, or whatever it is, but it's all those temptations.

[Here I am educating Brianna on how her mind works when she is in what we might loosely call her 'OCD state of mind' and what she needs to do when she recognises thoughts from this mind state – nothing!]

BRIANNA: Now you put it like that it's actually quite hard to imagine doing it differently, because listening to you I've now realised I've never done it differently. I've probably always had that OCD type of conversation about just this kind of thing.

WINDY: Yes, and I think that's probably served unwittingly to per-petuate it. I've got a little cartoon – I collect therapy cartoons – and there's one of this guy with guns and knives coming out of everything and there's a little person that is saying, "I sensed that I was in the presence of a person unused to rational discourse." That's what I'm calling your OCD mind. What's to be reasoned with? You reason with it, love that! Because it's coming from a place of doubt there's always something to say.

[This is a common intervention of mine – to indicate that various problems relish conditions that help maintain them. Here, OCD relishes attempts to reason with it, elsewhere anxiety relishes avoidance and attempts to eliminate it. Technically, what I am doing is helping a person to understand how they unwittingly maintain their problems.]

BRIANNA: Mmm. I'm aware that I'm anxious about the idea of letting go of it all, though, because that's interesting, because I can't imagine what that would be like not to have this ongoing discussion about that kind of thing.

WINDY: Because it's unfamiliar?

BRIANNA: Mmm.

WINDY: OK. What's anxiety-provoking about that unfamiliar state?

BRIANNA: Just because I can't imagine what I'd fill my head with. I don't know.

WINDY: Whatever you fill your head with when you have checked. You see? In other words you're doing other things.

BRIANNA: Yeah.

[In the next intervention, I use a technique from acceptance and commitment therapy (ACT) designed to show a person the impact of two ways of dealing with unwanted thoughts: one that strives to engage with it, the other designed to acknowledge its presence without engagement. Theoretically, what I am doing in this conversation is using REBT to encourage Brianna to develop a flexible attitude towards doubt, psychoeducation to help her understand how her mind works when she is in an OCD state of mind and ACT to encourage her to notice, but not engage with, thoughts that stem from that state of mind.]

WINDY: You see? It's a bit like holding something at arms' length. The way it's often put in the literature is that imagine that you and your friend have got two separate parties, right? And two smelly tramps gate-crash the parties. So, you've got one and the other one goes to your friend's. Now, at the friend's party, she's not a psychologist so they try to persuade the person to leave and they get angry with the person and they have a talk to the tramp, what do you think happens?

BRIANNA: Now I'm just transfixed with the idea, I don't want you to tell me I'd take the tramp in.

WINDY: No, no, no, no. Don't worry about that. This is not a sneaky way of getting a homework assignment.

BRIANNA: I don't know.

WINDY: Well, the tramp is going to dig their heels in. It's either going to be not responsive to reason and not responsive to be told what to do. You, however, are more astute in the field, so the best way to deal with this is to just ignore the tramp. Recognise that the person is there, obviously, but don't engage with them. After a while the tramp will get rather bored and go. It's exactly what happens. So, again, if you could say, "OK, I'm entering into an unfamiliar zone, I don't like it, I prefer the familiar, but I'm prepared to go boldly into that unfamiliar state," that Brianna has rarely been before. We're in a Star Trek type of a...

BRIANNA: Now you're trying to make me think it's all very funny, I can do this.

WINDY: Well, no, I think you can do it as long as you realise, realistically, you could do it with discomfort and unfamiliarity. You'll find out later how far you can do this comfortably, not the beginning.

BRIANNA: The thing that's really shocked me is the rationalisation, the 'talking myself through it' is actually part of the thing.

[I welcome this statement from Brianna. I want volunteers to be shocked because it indicates that they are learning something important.]

WINDY: Yeah.

BRIANNA: That's just never occurred to me before.

WINDY: That's right.

BRIANNA: I always thought that was me being really sensible and taking control of the OCD.

WINDY: Well, we actually used to think that in cognitive behavioural treatment of OCD, how likely is it that the bathroom's going to flood? And it's about as useful as saying to somebody with flying phobia, "How likely is it that the plane's going to crash?" while they're boarding the plane. That's not the kind of conversation you need to have with yourself. You need to understand what I call 'how the OCD mind works' and deal with it accordingly. Right?

BRIANNA: Yeah.

WINDY: Now, are you willing to do that?

BRIANNA: Yes.

WINDY: Good. So, I'm going to give you my email address and you can let me know how you get on.

BRIANNA: OK. Yes, thank you.

Follow-up

Four years and four months after the conversation with Brianna, she sent me the following to be used in this book.

I was keen to volunteer as a client to work with Windy for a therapy demonstration. I had been following his work for a number of years and I was interested to see if a brief session could make a difference. As we began, I knew that I trusted his expertise and I believe that expectation of benefit is key to a successful outcome regardless of approach. However, I think

I am also suited to Windy's style, ready to get to the nub of the issue without too much preamble.

My issues were real and bothersome. I had suffered from OCD for most of my life and, although I had managed to tackle some of the more distressing features, I was still struggling with some behaviours that were getting in the way of me leading a comfortable life. Essentially, the problem was my need to check my bathroom repeatedly.

Windy collected the relevant data, keeping me on track and homing in on the anxiety that kept the OCD going. Everyone loves to tell their own story but this takes time and, like most clients, I had told my story often. Rather than allowing me to indulge in this, Windy directed me carefully, respectfully and with good humour. We were soon at the first crucial moment. Windy asked for my goal which was to feel 'calm'. Windy explained that he couldn't help me with that in the short term and that, to feel better, I would have to tolerate an unpleasant or 'unpreferable' feeling. I realised that my efforts to stop the OCD had been perpetuating it. Only the OCD could help me to feel calm in the moment. I would need to work through situations with my anxiety and a sense of doubt in order to feel better.

The second breakthrough was Windy's explanation that my coping strategies to manage the OCD were part of the problem. I had thought that having a rational conversation in my head about the likelihood of my bathroom flooding was a good way to reduce the behaviours. He pointed out that anything I could argue would be countered by my OCD mind which would relish the challenge. Every time I would say "What are the chances..." my OCD mind would say "You never know," ramping up the doubt and anxiety. So the task was to step away from the OCD behaviours *and* the OCD thinking. Wow. I have to acknowledge that I was apprehensive agreeing to do the homework. Could it work for me? I agreed and went home in reflective mood.

I got out of my car and went indoors. The next morning, I realised that I hadn't needed to check the bathroom at all the previous evening or that morning. This was interesting and exciting, but it wasn't the best bit. I hadn't noticed the previous evening that I had walked into the house without going back to check my car doors were locked, another persistent behaviour. That one had disappeared with no effort at all. And, four years on, I can report that I am no longer troubled by a range of checking behaviours. I have no doubt at all that lasting work can be achieved in as little as 30 minutes. Thanks Windy!

Windy sent me the recording of the session the next day and I have played it for interested colleagues and counselling students. It has been useful to have a reminder although my experience was so powerful at the time that I haven't particularly needed to replay it to reinforce change. However, I can see that the opportunity to replay the session could be very helpful to clients.

Chapter 9

Anal sex without guilt...and alcohol: Leon

Length of conversation = 10 minutes and 47 seconds

Leon attended a UKCBT Meetup group on 11 May 2017. At these two-hour evening sessions, which are attended by a mixture of professionals and lay people, I begin the evening by giving a lecture on a particular theme (on this occasion, 'Guilt and Shame') followed by questions from the audience. Then, I usually have two conversations with members of the audience seeking help for a problem consistent with the theme of the evening. After each conversation, members of the audience can ask me or the volunteer questions about what they observed. This is what happened with Leon, who volunteered to engage in a conversation with me on his problem with guilt.

WINDY: OK, Leon, what problem can I help you with this evening?

LEON: I think that I suffer from chronic shame.

WINDY: Chronic shame, OK. Can you tell us a little bit about that in more detail, please?

LEON: Sure. I was born in the mid-50s when gay activity between men was illegal. I came out to myself at the age of 12, just as the law was changing, and really kept that very much to myself as much as I could, right the way through until I was 28. So I didn't come out until I was 28, properly. In the meantime, at university, I had a crisis, so severe depression, and was referred, initially, to the psychiatrist, who tried to convert me, unsuccessfully.

WINDY: To convert you?

LEON: To convert me to heterosexuality.

WINDY: Right. He'd be struck off today.

LEON: Yeah, indeed. Then a hypnotherapist had a go, and that didn't work either. I can still remember the opening line of every hypnotherapy session was, "Hey Leon, are you still a homo?" which was very affirming.

WINDY: Happy days!

[This is a humorously ironic remark. They were far from happy days. Leon understands what I am conveying to him.]

LEON: Indeed. So I seemed to achieve more equilibrium over time, but I wasn't really noticing the amount of alcohol I was consuming. I hit rock bottom in 2000, so 17 years ago, and really was in a situation there of total crisis, and it was when I decided that sobriety was the only way forward for me that I also realised that the only circumstances under which I could countenance a physical relationship was under the influence of alcohol.

WINDY: Which blocked what out?

LEON: Disinhibition, really. I mean there are sexual acts – I will spare everybody's blushes – that would make me feel uncomfortable, for example. So that disinhibiting effect, the alcohol did the trick, up to a point. Of course, it was a very negative way of coping. So, the dilemma I've faced since then is really whether or not I'm going to come to terms, at the age of 62 now, with living my life on my own and work on my own resilience, or whether I...

WINDY: Resilience for being on your own?

LEON: For being on my own, yes; for solitude. I don't mean isolation, but I mean solitude in terms of a relationship that's romantic or sexual. Or whether, in fact, this is something I should still work on. So that's the dilemma. I've tried various ways, which have been partly helpful, to disinhibit myself, such as regular mindfulness practice, and so on.

WINDY: And that disinhibits you by what?

LEON: It doesn't disinhibit to the point where I'm actually having any sexual relationships, and I still find the whole concept, actually, quite scary. So, in some ways, I feel as if I'm 62 intellectually, but, probably, emotionally, about 15, and that's difficult to come to terms...

WINDY: And, if we were successful this evening, what would we have achieved?

[Given the personal nature of the issue that Leon brought, I thought that it was important to allow him to express himself in his own way. Also, if shame is his problem, unfettered self-disclosure in front of a

group is important. Having given Leon such an opportunity, I decide to become goal-focused. This reveals that Leon is in a dilemma. Does he settle on being celibate or risk pursuing a sexual relationship where his fears and shame are activated?]

LEON: I would feel, whatever decision I made, whether it was to work towards being more resilient in a solitary life or whether it was better to be in a relationship, I feel that I was making a free choice. At the moment, I don't think I have the freedom to make that choice.

WINDY: Because your choice is being influenced by what?

LEON: I think my fears are too great for me to accept the second option at the moment.

WINDY: And the chronic shame, how does that fit in?

LEON: It's kind of paradoxical because I do a lot of active work within and beyond the LGBT community for gay rights and so forth, and equality, and, on the one hand, I'm able to give a lot of other people, I think, a lot of support around this, but, paradoxically, I find it very hard to turn the same trick on myself, if you like.

WINDY: So is the chronic shame pushing you in the direction of one fork in the road?

LEON: Yes.

WINDY: And which road is it?

LEON: That's the solitary one.

WINDY: That's the solitary one. So the solitary fork is being driven by fear and chronic shame.

LEON: It is, plus the fact there's familiarity there, because now, having spent more than a quarter of my life in a solitary existence and survived so far, I know I could. I'm pretty sure I could.

WINDY: Could what?

LEON: I could survive down that path. I'm not sure what the risks are, for example, of relapse if I go down the other route.

WINDY: Right, OK. So, if I helped you with your chronic shame, that would help you how?

LEON: Well, I think it would unlock a lot of the processes that are going on in my mind at the moment of running against brick walls.

WINDY: So what do you feel most shamed about?

LEON: I'm not shamed about my identity as a gay man and I feel quite comfortable to come into an environment like this, which is mixed, and share my sexual orientation. So, it's not that. I do feel shame around sexual activity, and that was also true when I had a one-off relationship with a girl; I also felt guilty about that.

WINDY: OK. So, I'm going to invite you to be as honest and free as you can, and they can take care of their own blushes, alright?

[This is a bit of a risky intervention. In order to do some meaningful work on Leon's shame problem – which is actually a guilt problem as we will see presently – I need him to be specific about 'A', the precise sexual behaviour he feels most ashamed/guilty about. Explicitly stating that he can do this and that the audience is responsible for their own responses to what he is prepared to discuss is my way of giving Leon 'permission' to be as honest as possible.]

LEON: OK.

WINDY: So what sexual acts do you feel most ashamed about, if I could help you deal with the shame, that might be something you could really take forward?

LEON: OK, well, for me, I've never been a receptive partner in anal sex, for example. I've been the active partner, again with a large amount of alcohol inside me. I wouldn't say it was something I was totally thrilled about. I think, even with the level of inebriation, I was still conscious that it didn't feel right. So I think there are issues around that. In terms of, if you like, activities that are probably more common to heterosexual and homosexual people, such as oral sex and other…

WINDY: OK, so what do you want to focus on: the anal or oral?

[This reads as very matter of fact. It is meant to! I want to convey that this is not an uncomfortable area for me, which it is not, and that it does not have to be an uncomfortable area for Leon. The audience members can take care of themselves!]

LEON: Let's go for anal.

[Leon's matter of fact response is encouraging for two reasons. He is expressing himself in a matter of fact way and I think that he has chosen the more difficult form of sexual behaviour to talk about.]

WINDY: So let's suppose that you are going to try anal sex as the penetrator. What, for you, is shameful about doing that?

LEON: I suppose it's a very basic notion of what the organs of the body are designed for and the notion that the anus is not designed, primarily, as a sex organ. So, unnatural, I suppose, the idea of unnatural.

WINDY: Alright, so let's suppose the act is unnatural. So you would be engaging in an unnatural act, let's suppose. Then what do you think you'd have to tell yourself about you, Leon, to create shame about engaging in that unnatural act?

[In both 'guilt' and 'shame', the extreme attitude of self-devaluation is to the fore. Thus, I use the 'let's assume that 'A' is true' strategy and focus on Leon's self-devaluation attitude. Interestingly, he responds with a rigid attitude. I use this to ask again for his self-devaluation attitude.]

LEON: Well, bluntly, "You must not commit an unnatural act."

WINDY: Because, if you do, what kind of person are you?

LEON: I'm not particularly religious, but sinful, I suppose, is the word I'd use.

WINDY: OK, so that's guilt.

['I'm a sinful person for doing something unnatural that I must not do' is a rigid attitude indicating guilt, not shame.]

LEON: Guilt, yeah.

WINDY: Let's suppose it is a sin, it's unnatural and sinful to act in that way, how does that make you a sinful person?

[Here, again, I invite Leon to assume temporarily that his 'A' is true, that anal sex is unnatural and sinful. I do this to highlight the most important determinant of his guilt, his extreme self-devaluation attitude: 'I am sinful'. It is this attitude that I am inviting Leon to question].

LEON: In a global sense?

WINDY: Yeah, because that's where guilt comes from.

LEON: Yeah, I don't think it does affect me in a global way.

[I could have made the point that while he does not think that he is sinful in a global sense, he does when he is focusing on his 'A' engaging in anal sex. What I do instead is to reinforce his emerging non-extreme

USA attitude. I do this by helping him to disconnect his 'self' from his so-called 'sinful' behaviour.]

WINDY: So why don't you practise that, try it and see how you go in reality, because you might like it, you might not, but, if you really practise that from saying, "I am not a sinful person, even though some people think this is sinful and some people think it's unnatural." Presumably other people don't, right?

[This last point is meant to provide a balance. Although we have assumed temporarily that engaging in anal sex is sinful, this is not a fact, but an opinion that some people hold, but others don't.]

LEON: Sure.

WINDY: So why couldn't you do that, without alcohol?

[I wish I had underscored this point at the end. Alcohol has served as a disinhibitor for Leon and it is important that he engages in anal sex, when he is ready to do so, free from its effects if he is going to get the full benefit of his developing non-extreme, USA attitude.]

LEON: I think the way you unpicked it actually made it seem far smaller an obstacle, because you've kind of fragmented it: it's not something like this, it's now a series of...

WINDY: Because I'm saying to you and asking you to invite yourself to see that the act doesn't identify you; you incorporate the act. How many other acts do you have to incorporate in this complex, fallible, very human organism called Leon? How many other acts do we have to include?

LEON: Well, quite a range, if you're talking about sexual activity, for example.

WINDY: Yeah. So you can practise anal sex, it doesn't define you unless you choose to allow it to define you.

LEON: So it's my choice?

WINDY: Yeah.

LEON: I take your point.

WINDY: A choice that's been...

LEON: It's been heavily conditioned by external factors.

WINDY: But, you see, you, as a human being, can recondition yourself. You don't have to be a slave to that conditioning, even though you still might like it, you might not.

LEON: But it puts me in a position of choice then, as well, doesn't it?

WINDY: That's right.

LEON: So that's a question of more freedom. That makes total sense, actually. That's very helpful.

[Leon is resonating to the idea that he has the freedom to choose his attitude and that, while he has been influenced by his conditioning, he does not have to be a slave to it.]

WINDY: So when can you put this into practice?

LEON: I can't give you a precise date.

WINDY: In CBT, we want specific times and dates.

LEON: It doesn't just involve me.

WINDY: Do you have somebody in mind?

LEON: Not at this moment, but I think, if I work on the concept and I think, also, if I bring some of this into my mindfulness practice, that would actually be a useful thing to do.

WINDY: Yeah. How would you do that?

LEON: Well, particularly focusing during a body scan, for example. During a full body scan you include the anus and you include the genitals, and so forth. I think, maybe, in my head, having more of a connection between the genitals and the anus would be a way of breaking down my own, if you like, internalised prejudice.

WINDY: Yeah, and to recognise that the totality of you, Leon, is not defined by your sexual activity.

[Here I am reminding Leon that he can do his 'body scan', focus on his anus and genitals and practise his non-extreme USA attitude as he does so.]

LEON: Yeah, sure.

Follow-up

That evening, Leon emailed me a few references of books that were mentioned in the audience discussion period after our conversation and added:

> Many thanks, too, for the brief 1:1 CBT session which I found remarkably powerful. It helped to fragment one of the major

barriers that has inhibited me from sexual contact in sobriety. I shall try the modification to my body scan meditation when I do my practice tomorrow.

Ten weeks later, when giving his permission for the material to be used here, Leon wrote the following:

> The most useful aspect of our session from my perspective was learning transferable skills from the process by which you guided me through one aspect of my dilemma around romantic and sexual relationships. The directness of your approach on the specifics of my squeamishness about anal sex was refreshing, and I feel that it successfully challenged my rationalisation about why I have always avoided being a passive partner.
>
> I have to say that my issues around relationships are far broader than this and I believe it would be unrealistic to tackle them in a single session. Some of the issues are:
>
> 1. Internalised homophobia – common in most gay men of my age. I pre-date the 1967 Sexual Offences Act. I could expand on this at length!
> 2. Fear of HIV infection – also common in gay men who lived through the initial HIV/AIDS crisis and who knew people who have died.
> 3. Fear of rejection – the gay community is ageist and focused on body image.
> 4. The prevalence of mental health issues in the gay community which makes it hard to find a stable partner.
>
> I'm hoping that tackling each of these issues on a self-help basis will enable me to resolve them. I'm finding the behavioural therapies helpful (REBT/CBT/ACT). I made good progress in tackling [general anxiety disorder] using CBT. ACT seems a good way to tackle my entrenched beliefs. (I recognise that my long abstinence from relationships is a good example of 'experiential avoidance'!)

Leon's subsequent feedback is important because it underscores the 'one thing' objective of a VBTC. Leon took from our conversation one important thing: his rationalisation about why he has always avoided being a passive partner was successfully challenged.

He recognises that there are a myriad of other issues that he needs to deal with and that they could not all be dealt with in one session. However, the fact that I could help him do the 'one thing' that he mentioned above was a step in the right direction for Leon as he embarks on a step-by-step journey to self-help.

Chapter 10

You can't turn a Romanian into a Chinese: Diane

Length of conversation = 16 minutes and 55 seconds

Diane attended a UKCBT Meetup group on 26 January 2017. At these two-hour evening sessions, which are attended by a mixture of professionals and lay people, I begin the evening by giving a lecture on a particular theme (on this occasion, 'Jealousy and Envy in Yourself and Others') followed by questions from the audience. Then, I usually have two conversations with members of the audience seeking help for a problem consistent with the theme of the evening. After each conversation, members of the audience can ask me or the volunteer questions about what they observed. This is what happened with Diane, who volunteered to engage in a conversation with me on her problem with jealousy that, as the conversation unfolded, turned out to be more of a problem with unhealthy anger.

There is a lot of humour in the conversation, which is not readily apparent from the transcript, but which comes through in the recording.

WINDY: OK, Diane, you wrote that you had a longstanding problem with jealousy.[1] Is that correct?

DIANE: Yes.

WINDY: OK. And you've tried to deal with it in a number of ways before?

DIANE: Yes. I've done personal development.

WINDY: What do you mean 'personal development'?

DIANE: So I've been to various seminars like Anthony Robbins' seminar, neurolinguistic programming, some CBT and spiritual work.

WINDY: And was any of that helpful to you in the longer term?

DIANE: Some of it, but I still have the negative emotions with jealousy.

WINDY: OK. Well, let's have a look at that a little bit more closely. Are you currently experiencing these emotions?

DIANE: Yes, absolutely.

WINDY: Do you want to tell us a little bit about that?

DIANE: …I cherish a normal, long-term, monogamous relationship.

WINDY: That's what you really want?

DIANE: Yes. And, eventually, get married to a soulmate. I have a friend or a part-time lover, but he wants a polyamorous relationship.

WINDY: And, by 'polyamorous', you mean that he is able to love more than one person at the same time?

DIANE: Yes.

WINDY: So he is polyamorous.

DIANE: Correct, and he wants me to be polyamorous.

WINDY: But you're not?

DIANE: Correct.

WINDY: Right.

DIANE: And I don't plan to.

WINDY: Fine.

DIANE: …And I met him about a year ago, last Valentine's.

WINDY: That's very romantic.

DIANE: But it won't be this Valentine's.

WINDY: What's his first name?

DIANE: Jim.

WINDY: I bet you he didn't say last year, "Hi, I'm Jim and I'm polyamorous," did he?

DIANE: …He didn't until I questioned him initially.

WINDY: When was that? On the 15th of February?

DIANE: After about a month or so.

WINDY: Why, because he was giving you some clues he might be?

DIANE: Correct, yes.

WINDY: And, when he said, "No, I'm polyamorous and I want a relationship with you but I want you to be polyamorous too," you said what?

DIANE: "Thank you but no thank you, please go away."

WINDY: So the going away was his responsibility.

DIANE: No, I asked him to go.

WINDY: So the going away was his responsibility, not yours? You didn't say, "Thank you but no thank you, I'm going away."

DIANE: I did try.

WINDY: That glue must've been pretty heavy.

DIANE: Normally I go with a guy. He's not that good looking; he's just average. He's like that 'whoopsy' guy that you were talking about earlier.

WINDY: Whoops, there's another rule: polyamorous people are not always attractive.

DIANE: But him and I have some kind of spiritual connection. Maybe that's why I'm going out with him.

WINDY: Fine, you're going out with him for the spiritual connection but what's your hidden agenda?

DIANE: The love-making's good.

WINDY: I didn't have that in mind. OK, the love-making is good and the spiritual connection is good.

DIANE: Yeah.

WINDY: But you're not accepting the terms of his offer, are you?

DIANE: Correct.

WINDY: So you're getting some of what you want but you're not getting all of what you want.

DIANE: Correct.

[I spend some time understanding the context of the problem before focusing more directly on its nature.]

WINDY: So when does the jealousy come in?

DIANE: The jealousy comes in when he makes appointments or dates with me and then he reschedules them or I'm expecting him to turn up at a certain time and he makes excuses and he shows up three hours later. I just find it unprofessional or disrespectful.

WINDY: Unprofessional? There's an association of polyamorous professionals, and part of the code of ethics is, when you make a date, you turn up on time. Do they have a sanction? Do you sanction these people? So unprofessional. Where does the jealousy come in?

DIANE: That he's putting another woman or other women before me.

WINDY: He may well be.

DIANE: Yeah.

WINDY: Yeah, and that means what to you?

DIANE: It creates the kind of negative emotions, not saying I'm not good enough, it makes me feel angry that he didn't deliver what he was supposed to deliver. He agreed on something.

WINDY: You're not the stranger that she's talking about?[2] First of all it seems you're not taking emotional responsibility. Who's creating the anger?

[Although Diane said that her problem was with jealousy, it is beginning to seem more a problem with unhealthy anger.]

DIANE: I am.

WINDY: Right, good. So his behaviour isn't. You are creating your own anger about his anger. Incidentally, all I can do is to help you feel badly about this guy's behaviour. Do you know why?

[I want to help Diane understand that it is healthy for her to feel bad, but not disturbed about her boyfriend's behaviour.]

DIANE: No.

WINDY: Because it's bad. He's not putting you first. We're assuming that, temporarily. What do you want to feel? Nothing about that or good about that?

DIANE: I want to feel normal. I don't want to feel disappointed, I don't want to feel that my stomach is churning upside down.

WINDY: Well, disappointed is normal, as far as I can see.

DIANE: But this is like more than normal. It's like down in the trench, and normally I'm a happy, positive type of person.

WINDY: And you're not saying this is an issue of self-worth?

DIANE: No. I love myself.

WINDY: Right, that's good. You can come in a few weeks and teach people how to do that. They struggle. So it's mainly anger because he's not doing what?

DIANE: Anger and disappointment, yeah.

WINDY: Because he's not doing what?

DIANE: Because he did not deliver what he promised.

[This appears to be Diane's adversity at 'A'.]

WINDY: And why does he have to deliver what he promises?

DIANE: Because he agreed, and that's the expectation I put on the situation.

WINDY: 'Expectation' is a bad word because it doesn't distinguish between prediction and insistence, right?…Rigid insistence. Do you mean, "When he promises, I predict he will deliver," or are you saying, "When he promises, I rigidly insist and demand that he deliver"?

DIANE: I'm OK if he reschedules it once or twice because things crop up, but, if he does it again and again. Previously, if he says 7 o'clock and changes it to 9 o'clock, I say, "OK, I'll go along with it," but this time I said, "No," and I didn't show up and said, "Not interested."

WINDY: Yeah, because you're saying, "I am prepared to accept a level of professional changing of the mind from somebody who's polyamorous, but this is unprofessional. It's too much."

DIANE: You're talking about the threat of loss. So I'm not afraid of losing him in the situation.

WINDY: No, but you're demanding that he has to deliver above the normal reasons why we change an arrangement.

DIANE: I come from a culture, in the Chinese culture if you say something, you do it. If not, then you tell the person ahead of time.

WINDY: Where does he come from?

DIANE: He comes from Romania.

WINDY: So the question is how to make a Romanian a Chinese. He's not a gypsy Romanian, is he? He's not a Roma?

DIANE: He's a professional Romanian.

WINDY: What does that mean?

DIANE: He works in IT.

WINDY: So the question is he doesn't go along with that rule. Your choice for you is to not like it but don't disturb yourself about it or to not like it and disturb yourself about it.

DIANE: I like him.

WINDY: No. Sorry, I'm not being clear. Your choice is to not like his behaviour, where he lets you down and doesn't follow through on promises more than is acceptable, it's to not like that and to disturb yourself about it or to not like it and not to disturb yourself about it. That's your choice. What are you doing at the moment?

[My intention here is to help Diane see that she has a choice between holding a rigid attitude or a flexible attitude towards her boyfriend's bad behaviour.]

DIANE: I try to let it not disturb me but it does, and that's the reality.

[Diane does not see the point I am making and retains the idea that the boyfriend's behaviour disturbs her. This is an 'A' causes 'C' connection which bypasses 'B', her rigid attitude.]

WINDY: No, you do. It doesn't, you do. My argument is that you're doing it by saying that, "I expect him to deliver on his promises and, therefore, he must. After all, that's what we do in China. If we do that in China, that's the way it has to happen in London with a Romanian." What do you think of that idea?

DIANE: ...[Pause]...

WINDY: Good idea or bad idea?...Bad idea. What are you going to change it to?

DIANE: Try not to let it disturb me.

[I am thinking at this point that Diane is not grasping the points I am trying to make. I am also aware that the evening is drawing to a close and that I am probably going to have to take more of a didactic stance.]

WINDY: Little vague. How are you going to do that?

DIANE: I know how to take responsibility of my own emotions but it's easier said than done.

WINDY: Well, it's easier said than done if you don't do it, right? In other words, if you're going with the grain is to say, "He's upsetting me," and that's the grain, and to go against the grain, which is difficult, is saying, "No, his behaviour's contributing but it's not creating my disturbance," and that goes against the grain.

DIANE: OK, so, when I own...the emotion, so, when I feel anger, in situations like this, what do I need to do? Do I go with anger, go with the flow?

WINDY: No, don't go with the flow because your anger is an unhealthy flow.

DIANE: Suppressed anger?

WINDY: Don't do that either.

DIANE: OK.

WINDY: Go to the source of the anger. Our theory says the source of the anger is not just, "I predict that he won't break his promises and, therefore," which is the real source of your anger, "he must not do so." That is with the grain. Going against the grain is, "Sadly and regretfully, no matter how they act in China, no matter how polyamorous he is or how good the love-making is, it doesn't follow that, when I want him to turn up on time, he has to do so. He doesn't." Why he's not is another matter, but we know the reality is he's not, and you're trying to, rather than change your attitude about reality, you're trying, through your rigidity, to change reality. That would be a good idea if he did because, if you sat there silently saying, "He's got to turn up on time, he promised, promised, promised," and there he is outside saying, "I'm in a polyamorous frame of mind, I'm off. A strange force is driving me back to Diane." That would make sense but does that happen? No. He has a mind of his own and your demandingness has no effect on his mind.

So the thing you need to accept, if you want to continue a relationship with him, is the following…you should have warned me of this because I would have brought two bottles of cod liver oil[3] for this one: (1) somebody who is polyamorous is going to want you to be polyamorous; he's not going to be monogamous. No matter how good the love-making is, it ain't gonna happen. (2) The reality is he is, at times, going to go off and do his own thing, even when he's promised to be in at the same time. That's not nice but he doesn't have to be the way you want him to be or the way that they are in China. It doesn't follow. If you can accept that, you then say, "Am I going to continue with this relationship under those conditions?"…Then you're going to have to deal with the other issue, which I probably haven't got time for: what's stopping you from walking away?

[Although I am talking slowly and with emphasis, although I am summarising the material that we have covered, it is clear that I am giving Diane too much to process in one go. However, I am also thinking that as I will send her the recording of the conversation and the transcript, she will be able to go over what I said in her own way and in her own time.[4]]

DIANE: …[Pause]…

WINDY: We'll deal with that next time.

DIANE: Yeah, that's what I'm trying to, walk away.

WINDY: Yeah, I know, but you're stopping yourself because the sex is good, because the energy's good, the spiritual connection is good.

DIANE: Yeah.

WINDY: Fine, and you'll be losing that, or you have it and you accept the grimness of the other stuff. So you're going to have to lose the spiritual connection. Now, that's not nice, but, if you can really say, "I don't need that stuff in my life, I can get it from somebody else who isn't polyamorous, who is a little bit more reliable, but it will mean me temporarily being without this guy." Now, if you're prepared to deprive yourself for a purpose, then that will be good. What do you think?

DIANE: Thank you.

WINDY: So have I succeeded where [neurolinguistic programming] has failed?

DIANE: Yes.

Notes

1 When signing up online to attend the UKCBT event, people are asked if they would like to volunteer for a conversation with me on a problem consistent with the theme of the evening. Diane said that she had a problem with jealousy, wanted help with this problem and was happy to volunteer to talk to me about it in front of an audience.

2 This is a reference to what another volunteer said in the previous conversation I had that evening.

3 A cod liver oil moment involves the volunteer swallowing something unpleasant because it is good for them in the long term.

4 This is what happened. Diane highlighted passages from the conversation that mean something to her. These helped her to end her relationship with her boyfriend.

Chapter 11

"I can do it even though I'm uncertain": Daphne

Length of conversation = 16 minutes and 33 seconds

Daphne attended a UKCBT Meetup group on 12 June 2017. At these two-hour evening sessions, which are attended by a mixture of professionals and lay people, I begin the evening by giving a lecture on a particular theme (on this occasion, 'Procrastination') followed by questions from the audience. Then, I usually have two conversations with members of the audience seeking help for a problem consistent with the theme of the evening. After each conversation, members of the audience can ask me or the volunteer questions about what they observed. This is what happened with Daphne, who volunteered to engage in a conversation with me on her problem with procrastination.

WINDY: What's your first name?

DAPHNE: Daphne

WINDY: OK, Daphne, how can I help you with your procrastination problem today?

DAPHNE: We talked about it,[1] whether it was around procrastination or kind of overwhelming. I take on too many things, and then I'm not very good at prioritising. So I'm good at the work that I do, but doing the work that I do requires me to run a business, which I'm not good at, and I get very overwhelmed.

WINDY: What's your goal in bringing this up with me this evening?

DAPHNE: ...[Pause] Seeing if I can gain more insight and clarity and find a space where I can break through some of the murkiness that exists in this for me.

[I note to myself the vagueness of Daphne's goal, so I decide to see if I can get greater clarity on her problem.]

WINDY: OK, so, you're saying you may take on too much, right? Does that help you solve the problem of procrastination or does it help to create the problem of procrastination?

DAPHNE: It helps to create it, and one of the things in the break, when we spoke,[2] that I realised was, you asked me whether, if I didn't take on too much, I would be able to not procrastinate, and I said I don't know. One of the things that that made me realise is I don't think there's ever been a time in my adult life where I haven't taken on too much.

WINDY: And when you say 'too much', what's the 'too' in the equation?

DAPHNE: ...[Pause] I'm very interested in a lot of things, and my sense is I have a fear of letting go of things that I enjoy or things that bring me something. So I'm just not good at letting go of them, so I think...I understand from other people, and I'm beginning to believe this, that you have to focus on fewer things, because each area takes a lot of work to develop.

WINDY: OK, so are we talking about you giving up something that you enjoy at the moment because it really isn't in your interest to keep it on because of your business or other aspects that you want to do, or are we talking about you saying no to things that are coming in that sound quite interesting that you don't want to say no to?

DAPHNE: We're talking about me giving up areas of my business development so that I can focus on other areas.

WINDY: Right, and you see that it is in your interest to do that?

DAPHNE: Reluctantly, yes.

WINDY: You reluctantly realise that you need to give it up or you reluctantly see that doing so is in your interest? I'm not quite sure where the reluctance is.

DAPHNE: ...[Pause] Both, actually. I'm somewhat reluctant to see it, but, now that I've seen it, I am reluctant to do it.

[Helping someone with their procrastination problem does require working with a specific example of the problem, which I now do.]

WINDY: OK, can you think of something that you are reluctant to give up that it would be in your interest to give up? Let's be specific.

DAPHNE: ...[Pause] Yes.

WINDY: What is that thing that you're reluctant to give up?

DAPHNE: ...[Pause] I'm a partner in a law firm where I head up their mediation division, and it just sucks a lot of my time and I have to get involved in many other things.

WINDY: It's like a hoover.

DAPHNE: It's like a hoover, yes.

WINDY: And you have no active voice here.

DAPHNE: You're right. You're right...[Pause] I have to get involved in other things in order to fulfil my role, and I don't find them fulfilling; they're not central to my role and I...feel...is it passive if I say I feel like my energy gets drained?

WINDY: By what?

DAPHNE: By getting involved in all these things.

WINDY: Well, it's a consequence that you have drained energy. Let's put it like that. Is it in your interest to give up this work to concentrate on what you consider to be the more important aspects of your business?

DAPHNE: There's a fear in me when I think of giving it up that it won't be in my interest in the longer term, and I'm not sure that's right. It's possibly just a fear. In the shorter term it feels like...I have an uncertainty around whether I can grow personally big enough to be able to handle all and everything else that I do, or whether it is in my interest just to give it up.

WINDY: But, if you did give it up, you would have the time and the energy to devote to these other aspects of your business so that you'll at least know whether or not you made the right decision to give it up later, if you were to give it up.

[Daphne is reluctant to do this experiment and as, she notes below, doing so means taking the risk of making a mistake.]

DAPHNE: Yes. So I'd have to risk making a mistake.

WINDY: That's right, and how do you feel about possibly giving up this work and it proves that, it turns out to be the wrong move?

DAPHNE: I'd feel terrible about it.

WINDY: Terrible in what way?

DAPHNE: ...[Long pause]

WINDY: What's the feeling?

DAPHNE: So, actually, the first feeling I have, when I think about giving it up, is relief...And then there's an element of worry and there is something, also, around my self-esteem. There is something around...[Long pause] There is a part of me that feels like giving it up would mean that I was failing at something, and there is a part of me that...[Long pause] I am questioning whether I would...[Pause] I'm questioning the outcome, I'm questioning whether I would be able to do what I want to do on my own without the link with this organisation, even though it's not proved very helpful so far.

WINDY: So, on the one hand, you may have to deal with failing, and on the other hand you're dealing with the uncertainty of whether it would be right. Which do you think is the major block to giving it up? Dealing with failing or dealing with the uncertainty of not knowing whether it's the right decision or not?

DAPHNE: The uncertainty.

[This is quite a complex issue, but I am keen to help Daphne drill down and focus on the major block, which she nominates as uncertainty about what will happen if she gives up unfulfilling aspects of her work. I will now work with this focus and help Daphne to do so as well.]

WINDY: OK, so, at the moment, if you gave it up, you suspect it will help you to concentrate your focus on your business, but you don't know for sure, right?

DAPHNE: And there may be other options in between giving it up and not giving it up.

WINDY: Yeah, but if I can help you to at least clear the block to giving it up, that would at least help you with that particular option, even though it's not an option that you'd necessarily take; at the moment you're not considering it truly because you've got a block about that. So let's have a look at what we know. We know that you want to know that, if you gave it up, it would be the right thing. Is that right? Do we know that?

DAPHNE: Yes...yes, and, tell me if I am changing tack and I'm sure you will feel free to bring me back.

WINDY: I'll feel very free to bring you back, yeah.

[Note the humour between the two of us about my role in maintaining the focus.]

DAPHNE: But I think where the procrastination also comes in is taking the steps to do whatever it is I need to do to even begin to give it up.

WINDY: What steps are they?

DAPHNE: …I have to sit down and write a letter and set out options and I have to choose what I want.

WINDY: How are you stopping yourself from doing that?

DAPHNE: …[Pause] My idea is that I need to know what option I want before I start to write.

WINDY: So we're back still with the idea of you'd like to know in advance the outcome of your decision. That's fine. You'd like to know you're doing the right thing.

[I note that this change of tack is really another example of the same problem that Daphne has with not knowing in advance what option she wants before she examines all the options.]

DAPHNE: Yeah.

WINDY: OK, that's fine. The question is not why you'd like to know it, but (a) do you need to know, or (b) do you not need to know?

[Now I cut to the attitudinal chase. I ask whether her attitude about uncertainty is rigid or flexible. Note that she does not answer the question, but I refuse to move away from the attitudinal focus that I have created.]

DAPHNE: Well, I can't know.

WINDY: Well, that's not the question. I didn't say can or can't you. I'm saying is it necessary or is it desirable but not necessary, in reality?

DAPHNE: Well, it can't be necessary because it's not possible. It's not possible to know the outcome of any decision.

WINDY: But people still demand to know things that they can't possibly know. That's human beings for you.

DAPHNE: So it's not necessary.

WINDY: So which one are you operating on at the moment, in terms of your procrastination?

DAPHNE: I'm operating as if it's necessary.

WINDY: That's right. If you operated it, in reality, that it's not necessary but desirable, it would be nice to know, but it's not necessary, at least you'll sit down and do the thinking and really do the planning and see what's happening. But, at the moment, you're putting that off because, as far as I can hear, you're saying, "I need to know what's the outcome of all of this before I really get to grips with it," which is exactly the thing that we talked about, the other thing. You said, "I've got to know what's going to happen if I give this up." So my hypothesis is that you have a very human desire to know, but then your active choice is to really ask yourself, "Do I need to know this or is it desirable but not necessary?" And which one of those is going to really help you to get to grips with "the work I need to do, the thinking that I need to overcome my procrastination"?

[It is important in working with problems with procrastination to help the person see the link between their rigid attitude to, in this case, uncertainty and their avoidance behaviour and the link between their flexible attitude towards the same adversity and overcoming their problem. Note that this is what I have just done with Daphne.]

DAPHNE: So it's desirable but not necessary.
WINDY: Right. Now how are you going to apply that to the next time you sit down, which is when, by the way? When are you going to choose to sit down and work this one through, because I forgot to mention in the lecture, working with procrastination, you have to pin people down to a place and time. So what are you going to opt for?
DAPHNE: To have a break every week.
WINDY: I'm sure you do.
DAPHNE: Can we put off the 'when' for a moment? Is that OK?
WINDY: As long as you realise that I'm going to bring it back.
DAPHNE: Yes.
WINDY: So let's put it off for a moment.
DAPHNE: My sense is I need to sit down and I need to be uncomfortable.
WINDY: Correct.
DAPHNE: I needed to say that. That's important.

[Daphne has stressed for herself something that I was going to emphasise. It is more important for the volunteer to do this than for me to do it in that she is more likely to take away the point if she has highlighted it before I do.]

WINDY: Right, definitely. The discomfort that goes along with being uncertain.
DAPHNE: Yeah, and the discomfort that goes along with not knowing how what I write and how what I put down will be received and perceived.
WINDY: That's right.

DAPHNE: Not being able to control all the outcomes in everyone else's mind.

WINDY: That's right. The only thing that you can control is what you are the author of.

DAPHNE: Yeah.

WINDY: So can we bring the 'when' back? Have you said what you wanted to say? OK, let's bring the 'when' back. When are you going to do this?

[Without wanting to 'rain on Daphne's parade', I bring the discussion back from the general point to a specific application of that point. General learning without specific application is not as good as general learning with specific application for long-term outcome.]

DAPHNE: ...[Pause] At the latest, this weekend.

WINDY: OK, let's be a little bit more precise what 'at the latest' means. Are we talking about Saturday? Sunday? Friday?

DAPHNE: Saturday.

WINDY: What time Saturday?

DAPHNE: As I fly to Amsterdam on Saturday, that's the latest time, and as I'm travelling.

WINDY: You're going to do this on the aeroplane?

DAPHNE: That was the latest.

WINDY: OK, and when's the earliest?

DAPHNE: The earliest is tomorrow afternoon.

WINDY: OK, so what do you want to commit yourself to? The earliest or the latest? What's in your best interest?

DAPHNE: It's in my best interest to do it earlier rather than later.

WINDY: So tomorrow afternoon.

DAPHNE: Yes, although I have stuff planned, but I...[Pause] I guess I could start around 1 tomorrow afternoon.

WINDY: OK, so here's a little tip and a technique – could you replace 'around' with 'at'?

['At' is more precise than 'around' and, with people with a longstanding problem with procrastination, specificity is key.]

DAPHNE: Well, I would rather start earlier and there's a possibility I could start earlier.

WINDY: OK, so the latest would be 1 o'clock, OK?

DAPHNE: Yes.

WINDY: OK, and how long will this take you, do you think?

DAPHNE: ...Well, I have a meeting at 4:15.

WINDY: OK, so you've got three-and-a-quarter hours at the minimum, right?

DAPHNE: Hmm mmm [yes].

WINDY: So what I want you to imagine is that you start whatever time you start and I want you to imagine that you start to be uncomfortable, right? So, you start and then you recognise, "OK, I'd like to know the outcome of all this, but I have a choice whether I decide that I need to know it or I don't need to know it." You can choose at that point. If you choose to turn it into a necessity, you're procrastinating. If you choose to keep it as a flexibility, you'll continue it, even though it will be uncomfortable. That's your choice.

[Here, I use imagery rehearsal with an adversity focus – uncertainty-related discomfort and a choice between her rigid attitude and her flexible attitude.]

DAPHNE: ...Sounds good.

WINDY: Can I help you make that choice or have you already made it?

DAPHNE: I've already made it.

WINDY: Good. Congratulations.

DAPHNE: Thank you.

Notes

1 When people sign up to attend a UKCBT Meetup group, they are asked to say if they would like to volunteer for a problem-focused conversation consistent with the theme of the evening. When there are more than two volunteers, I ask these people to see me in the break so I can choose two people with a relevant problem. If there are more than two, I select them on a first come, first served basis.

2 See Note 1.

Chapter 12

"I am not defective": Lily

Length of conversation = 24 minutes and 28 seconds

Lily attended an evening session I gave at the 'Society of Psychotherapy' held at the Existential Academy in North West London on 20 June 2017. I gave a short lecture on 'Very Brief Therapeutic Consultations: What Can Be Achieved?' The event was advertised as follows: "In this session, I will discuss what might be gained from very brief therapy consultations of 30 minutes or less. I will demonstrate how I work in this modality with volunteers from the audience wishing to be helped with genuine concerns. This work will then be discussed by those present." As time was limited, I only had an opportunity to have one conversation – with Lily.[1]

WINDY: OK, Lily, what particular issue can I help you with this evening?

LILY: As I was coming here tonight, I thought it might be a really good idea to have an opportunity to get a different perspective on something that I'm having difficulty with. Several years ago, I was diagnosed with MS, and I'm finding that really quite difficult to manage. Normally I'm OK and I'm in remission at the moment. So, when I'm in a relapse, obviously I start, there's an issue with body image because how I am is suddenly not who I become. I have difficulty with walking, maybe vision, and it can get really severe, at those times when I'm walking along. So sometimes I have a stick, but I've gradually…I can't say I've got used to it, but it helps me to walk. Where I have a difficulty is, I have a very deep feeling in myself that's gradually increasing that people won't want to know me in those moments.

WINDY: In those moments when?

LILY: When they sort of see who I've suddenly changed into, kind of Jekyll and Hyde.

WINDY: Are you saying that people that you know won't want to know you or people that are strangers to you?

LILY: I don't know. It's really difficult because I don't know if anyone has a stick or if they've experienced walking outside, because people are really horrible outside. The longer you have what I would call a disability, you get to realise that there's a whole thing that goes on in public where I've had people literally kick the stick away, and I gradually get to know that other people have experienced this, and I even read it the other day. I was really surprised, and I thought that might just be happening to me, but other people are out there. I just struggle with how people suddenly see me when I go into this other state. My friends even though I might think they might not like me when they see the other side of me that normally isn't.

WINDY: You mentioned, at the beginning, that you were interested in perhaps a different perspective.

[I am aware that Lily has given me a lot of very personal information very quickly. I am looking for a way of developing a goal-orientated perspective while being sensitive to the material that Lily has disclosed. So, I pick up on something that she said at the outset about wanting a different perspective.]

LILY: Yes.

WINDY: What perspective do you have on this at the moment that you are wondering if there was a different way of looking at it?

[I want to understand how she see things now and her ideas about what might constitute a different perspective.]

LILY: Yeah, I think because you were saying about different perspectives…I don't know, I suppose it's a really difficult one tonight because it's not something that I can change in myself.

WINDY: What can't you change?

LILY: There's no cure for MS at the moment.

WINDY: No, so you can't change your MS.

LILY: Yeah, I can't change that.

WINDY: And you can't change other people's reactions.

LILY: Yeah, I can't change their reactions as they're walking along the streets.

WINDY: What about your reactions to their reactions?

[My goal here is to clarify with Lily what she can't change – her MS and others' reactions to her – and what she can change – her reactions to their reactions.]

LILY: Well, I'm sort of learning.

WINDY: You are?

LILY: Yeah, generally.

WINDY: What are you learning?

LILY: I try to say to myself they don't matter. I've got friends.

WINDY: Sorry, they don't matter?

LILY: Yeah, like…I don't know, like that lady was saying about a stammer, they said, "Who cares?" Not who cares, but it doesn't matter if you have a stammer. I just think I should be thinking, "Well, I'm still me," but people would react differently to me, somehow.

[Lily has tried the perspective of 'indifference', which is problematic, since how people react to her does matter. I am thinking that I need to help her focus on a specific adversity and help her deal constructively with this.]

WINDY: So you're still you.

LILY: Yeah, I've just got this overwhelming gradual feeling.

WINDY: So you're trying to convince yourself that it doesn't matter if?

LILY: I suppose it shouldn't matter. If I saw somebody…

WINDY: What shouldn't matter, Lily?

LILY: …I suppose it shouldn't matter what…not what people think, but…I should be more self-assured to think, "Well, I'm me," instead of feeling…

WINDY: Have you been trying to convince yourself that it shouldn't matter how people might treat you?

LILY: Yeah, I suppose I have.

WINDY: And what successes have you had?

LILY: Probably none.

WINDY: Do you understand why?

LILY: No. Maybe I'm approaching it in the same way.

WINDY: Well, I'm hearing that it does matter to you and that you're trying to convince yourself that what matters to you shouldn't matter to you.

LILY: ...

WINDY: Does that make sense?

LILY: Yes.

WINDY: So I wonder what would happen if you could...I guess it depends how you end the sentence, also, about, "Look, this matters to me," meaning that, "It's important for me that other people..." what?

LILY: ...Perhaps recognise, although, if they're a stranger, they wouldn't recognise who I am.

WINDY: Right.

LILY: ...I think, inside, there's a thing in me of a conflict between who I was, what I was able to do, as opposed to when I get a relapse. Obviously, I can't do the things that I know I can do normally.

WINDY: Yeah.

LILY: There's a massive divide. So, when you walk along a street or even friends – I haven't actually told some friends what I actually have because I'm worried about their reaction.

[I am aware that Lily is raising two different, but related concerns: how she deals with others' abusive reactions to her and how she deals with the person she used to be and the person she is when she has an MS relapse. I am aware that I don't have the time to help her with both and if I don't help her to focus on one then I may help her with neither, so I summarise what she has said and use that summary to help her focus.]

WINDY: OK, let me feed back what I'm hearing, because I think it's important to see which bit of it you would like to focus on. There's a bit about dealing with other people – "Should it matter to me?" "Shouldn't it matter to me?"; but there's also the bit that I'm hearing about your relationship with you – "Am I the same person when I can walk?" "Am I the same person when it's more difficult?" Which bit would you like to focus on, if that's a meaningful distinction?

LILY: I think me, because then, if I can deal with that, maybe I can...

WINDY: OK, so it's your relationship with you.

LILY: Mmm [yes].

WINDY: OK, so tell me a little bit about how that changes according to how your symptoms might fluctuate.

LILY: As in?

WINDY: In terms of the MS.

LILY: What I think about me?

WINDY: Yeah.

LILY: ...I think, because it was so dramatic, the way that it happened, which I was in a wheelchair at one stage and gradually got back up, with a lot of physio and stuff. And now I've got medication to help, which is fantastic, after going on a clinical trial only five years ago, so it enables me to be who I am now. But...I don't know, what was the question, sorry?

WINDY: In terms of how you view yourself, your relationship with you. It sounds like there are times when you can walk and times when you can't.

LILY: Yes.

WINDY: How your viewpoint about yourself changes.

LILY: Yeah, I get frustrated, because what I want to do I can't do. Then I suppose I feel quite, not ashamed, but I don't know if I am ashamed, I just suddenly get really...feel depressed because suddenly I then have to turn people down who I might have gone out with or something, because I can't physically go out, so that's always very upsetting. You have to do it with a moment's notice, so people might not understand, but I've kind of worked with that one. I can't change that.

[Lily has chosen to focus on her relationship with herself when she relapses. She mentions depression and shame, so I try to get her to drill down and focus on one of these reactions.]

WINDY: Do you want to focus on the shame bit or the depression bit of how you view yourself?

LILY: ...I suppose the shame, maybe.

[I note Lily's halting response, but decide not to say anything yet to see what unfolds.]

WINDY: So what would you say, when you are ashamed, what are you ashamed about?

LILY: I just don't understand how I've come to that situation, where nobody in my family had it. I don't know if it is shame. It just feels really depressing and...yeah.

WINDY: So you're not sure if it's shame you experience...or whether it's depressing that you can't understand why this has happened to you.

LILY: I don't know. It's complicated, isn't it?

WINDY: OK, I'm keen for you to take away something. I'm mindful of what you said about taking away a new perspective. So I think it's useful if we can just focus on an area where you might value a different perspective. So, if I can just summarise, we spoke, initially, about how to deal with people's reactions to you and when it becomes obvious that you've got a stick and you can't walk, particularly when people can be quite cruel and abusive. We're talking about how your view of you might change. And now we're talking about whether you're experiencing shame or depression. So there's a lot there, right? So what I'm keen to offer you is an opportunity to focus on one element of this experience, which might help you to take away one thing that might make a difference to you. If you were to choose a particular focus of all the ones that we've spoken about, what might it be?

[Once again, I provide a summary, one that is more detailed than my previous one, and this time I bring back the idea of a 'different perspective'. I ask her directly to choose a particular focus for the rest of our conversation.]

LILY: I think, because it has a knock-on effect, I think because the way people treat you when they see it, that inwardly impacts, and then I get frustrated and then I feel shame.

WINDY: So would it be useful if I helped you with a different perspective about how other people treated you, at the beginning of the process?

LILY: Yes.

[We have now agreed to focus on Lily's response to others' treatment of her. I am hoping that this focus may take root, so I ask for an example of this problem.]

WINDY: So can you give me an example of what you're talking about here, in terms of when somebody treated you in a way that it started to impact on how you viewed yourself?

LILY: Yeah, I think I was walking along with a stick. Well, there are two incidences. Somebody came up, kicked the stick away and then spat on me, and said whatever they said, because I was, in their eyes, perhaps disabled. There was another one where I was actually in a wheelchair, and I went to a Paul Weller concert, who I love, and a group in their 30s, probably, group of people who should've known better, just came up and said, "Look at that spaz,"[2] and literally surrounded me. That was my first experience of looking different.

[Lily reports two incidents, so I ask her to focus on one.]

WINDY: So which one shall we focus on in our discussion?

LILY: I think the one with the stick, because I'm not in a wheelchair. So, the stick I usually sometimes do have.

WINDY: So they kicked your stick and they spat on you.

LILY: Yes.

WINDY: Did you fall down?

LILY: No. Luckily there was a pole there.

WINDY: And did they say anything else?

LILY: No, just walked off.

WINDY: OK, so how were you left feeling and thinking?

LILY: I felt pretty awful at that point.

WINDY: Can you tell us a bit more about that?

LILY: I don't know. I felt like crying, and then I felt like shouting at them, and then I thought I'd better not because they might come back.

WINDY: What did you feel like shouting?

LILY: Just like, "How dare you do that to someone?" I think, if I saw that happen…

WINDY: And outrage.

LILY: Yeah, so that was really difficult.

WINDY: So that was focused on them.

LILY: Yeah.

WINDY: You were outraged. How about the bit where it left you feeling about yourself?

LILY: Yeah, I think I had to double-check myself – am I OK, I haven't fallen down.

WINDY: Sure, but in terms of…

LILY: I just, inside, curled up a bit and thought, "Oh God."

WINDY: Oh God what?

LILY: "What just happened?" and then I just carried on walking because I thought, "Well, I can't do anything, really." I do try to reframe things, if I can, so I thought, "Well, alright."

*[I am aware that I haven't helped Lily to express her emotional response
to this event. My guess is that she tries to 'reframe' things too quickly,
partly as a way of coping with her distressed emotions. I use the word
'frame' to bridge to her feelings.]*

WINDY: First of all, what was the frame that you experienced that
you then tried to reframe, because I'm not quite clear about what
that left you feeling about yourself?

LILY: I just felt a bit ashamed, really. I don't know. Maybe that
I couldn't walk properly enough for them not to notice.

WINDY: OK. So their very dramatic and crude and abusive reaction
was a fairly vivid reminder of things that you couldn't do.

LILY: Yeah, I think I was just trying to master the walk and trying to
look confident and trying to be confident with the stick as much
as you can be, and pace it and balance, and everything else. It
took a lot. From here to the front door might have taken me
about 20 minutes, 25 minutes, to walk at that stage.

WINDY: OK. Would you be interested in a particular perspective
about shame that you might find useful that might help, at least
to understand around it?

*[I am aware of the passing of time at the moment so I decide to take
the theme of 'shame' and ask Lily if she would like to hear a perspective
on shame that might be helpful to her.]*

LILY: I think so.

WINDY: So shame tends to be an emotion that people struggle with,
obviously, but it tends to be based on one of either three types
of self-devaluations. One is, 'I'm defective', the other one is, 'I'm
disgusting', and the other one is, 'I'm diminished'. I wonder if
that framework, any of those three that you might resonate with
or you might say, "No, it's not that, it's this." Do any of those
three ring a bell in terms of what your experience was?

LILY: I think one of the three.

WINDY: OK. You'll have to help my ageing brain here.

LILY: I'm diminished. That was the third one.

WINDY: Yeah.

LILY: What was the first one?

WINDY: Defective and disgusting.

LILY: I don't think I'm disgusting. I haven't got to that bit yet, but
I am defective.

WINDY: And you're defective. Which of those two do you think was more to the fore?

LILY: Defective.

WINDY: Defective, OK. So...they treated you in a very dramatic, abusive way, and part of your experience is focused on them, "How dare you?" but part of you started to think that, "I'm defective and I'm showing the world that I'm defective"...Have you tried to reframe that 'I'm defective' or is this the first time that you've really focused on that?

LILY: Yes, this is the first time I've focused on it, really.

[This shows that Lily's attempts to reframe have not got to the heart of the matter. This is that she feels shame (at 'C' in the Situational ABC framework discussed in Chapter 5) because she thinks she is defective (at 'B') in the face of the adversity of being abused (at 'A').]

WINDY: So...

LILY: And you gradually become more and more defective, every time it happens, which is quite mind-bending.

WINDY: OK, I'm going to give you a personal experience, and I want you to focus on the...not on the content, but on the example. It's another one of stammering, actually, because the other thing that I learnt, and I don't know where I learnt it from, is that I found out that it was very important to me, psychologically, to distinguish between 'I'm a stammerer' and 'I'm a person who stammers some of the time and is fluent some of the other time', OK? Now, how do you react to that distinction – 'I'm a stammerer' versus 'I'm a person who stammers some of the time and doesn't stammer at other times'? What, for you, is the distinction between those two statements?

[I decide at this point to use self-disclosure to help Lily examine her extreme self-devaluation. I would usually ask Lily for permission to do so, but the example refers to stammering, to which Lily referred earlier, so I thought she would resonate with the point.]

LILY: The word 'person'.

WINDY: OK. In the first one, what I learnt was, the more I identified with the stammering, that I am a stammerer, it became an identity for me, and, actually, I stammered more, because what do people who stammer do? To actually stammer more.

I'm wondering if one perspective might be, rather than, 'I'm defective', 'I'm a person who is, some of the time, in this area, I can walk, and some of the time I struggle, but also I have all these other aspects of me that are not touched by my MS'.

LILY: ...I think it's when it becomes visible, that's when it becomes difficult for me.

WINDY: Yeah, indeed.

LILY: Even more difficult.

WINDY: Indeed.

LILY: And everyone can see it.

WINDY: And that's why I think your perspective becomes more relevant when it becomes more visible. So...I wonder if you can actually focus a little bit more about this and imagine that, when you're not walking well in public with a stick and you're struggling, and people might notice, that you take out for a walk the idea that you're defective; this proves that you're defective. Can you imagine doing that, however painful that is?

LILY: I don't know because it's ever-present.

WINDY: Yeah, I mean you're doing that anyway, it sounds like, but I wonder if you can also imagine taking out the idea, and actually responding, because it's natural to have that initial reaction, 'I am defective', but, if you can actually watch for that, and this is the choice: you can either choose to continue that or to say, "Actually, no, I'm not going to define myself or be defined by my MS. I have it, but I'm much more of a person. I may be deficient in this walking aspect, but I am not defective as a person." I wonder if you can imagine responding to your defective narrative with that more complex, more accurate. Which do you think is true, by the way? That you're defective or that you're a very complex person who can't be defined by her MS, even though it's visible?

[Here I make the point that her first response, 'I'm defective', is to be expected. The important issue is that she responds to this attitude with a more constructive alternative.]

LILY: Yeah, but people have said to me, "Oh, you're so much more than that," but I think, if you have it, suddenly your whole world changes; your perspective changes.

WINDY: Yeah, I'm not saying your whole world doesn't change. I'm just saying what constant can you hold on to? What truth about yourself? Not the fact that your world's going to change.

Of course it's going to have changed. You now live in the world where some people are going to be nasty enough to treat you abominably. So your world has changed. But I'm wondering, if you held onto something constant and accurate about you, what difference that might make to you.

[I am referring to the constant of her attitude towards herself she can hold on to.]

LILY: So, if people do anything, then I can just think, "Well, I'm still…more than that."

WINDY: But to allow yourself to care about how you're treated by other people, because you're trying to persuade yourself not to care about something you deeply care about.

[So, I am encouraging her to care about how she is treated, but to hold on to the idea that she is more than she is treated.]

LILY: I hadn't actually thought that until you said it.

WINDY: Yeah, so it's about, "Can I hold on to an aspect of myself, when I catch myself responding that I'm defective? No, I'm not." You can actually put it in your own words, but what I'm trying to get at is the complexity of you as a human being, that, yes, your world has changed in terms of how you're treated, but that you can choose to define yourself as you are: a complex, myriad human being whose world has changed, but certain things are constant, and that you can care about how you're treated by people. I wonder if that might be something that would fit the bill of taking away a different perspective.

LILY: …That's quite amazing, actually, because I hadn't actually thought of that.

[Her last two responses show an emotion-based recognition of what I am saying and this may well represent the different perspective that she was seeking.]

Follow-up

Three weeks after the interview, when I sent Lily the digital voice recording and the transcript, I received a brief email in which she said the following:

I have received your transcript and recording. It really is 'quite something' to see in print, and I have now listened to the recording 3 times already! It is compelling to hear, and to read, and I am understanding a little more each time I think about our conversation. I even had a thought come to me as I was walking along the road the other day, and straightened up a little as to how I was walking along. As I felt a little 'taller' I started to look at people, and one person smiled at me. I don't know what she was smiling at me for, but it felt good!

Then, just over four months after the interview, in response to my invitation to write about her experience of our VBTC, Lily wrote the following:

I am looking forward to reading the other conversations in the book, but think I will initially feel a bit nervous when I read my own. Perhaps reading it 'in-print' in an actual book, I think will somehow make my difficulty kind of real. Maybe, it is because I now realise that I acknowledged for the first time (during my conversation with Windy on that evening), how it makes me feel when my usually 'invisible' illness becomes visible to others. Also, when people react negatively toward me on those occasions.

A bit of background

I had struggled with the whole concept of having MS, and learning to live with it. It was especially hard when my walking became difficult. Months went by until one day when with my friend, I broke down in tears. After much silence, I eventually told him that I had 'forgotten' how to walk. It felt like a kind of confession. You never think you will forget how to walk. If any reader has experienced this, they will know this to be quite profound.

The next day, I asked my friend to walk while I watched, in the hope of remembering the action of walking. I started making drawings of his feet walking, the angle of movement, where they first touched the ground, to help me remember. He was very patient over the next few weeks as I did this. I decided to combine my task of walking again with something that I enjoyed. I remembered a Photographer, Eadweard Muybridge, who had taken photographs of Horses in the 1800s to study the motion of how they ran. I too tried to capture the motion of my friend's feet, and putting the images together, I made a flip-book. It now showed me a step-by-step guide as to how to move my feet and legs. The day came for me to venture outside for the first time. However, I started to learn that venturing outside was very different from the privacy of learning to walk in my own way, at home. I encountered a group on the street who approached me. They started to point and laugh, and called me derogatory names. Their actions amplified my vulnerability at my clumsy attempts to walk. I felt embarrassed and ashamed. Another day, a man angrily kicked my stick out of the way, and spat on me as they passed by. I was in their way. An on-going catalogue of similar events ensued, not every time that I went out, but gradually, which added to my feelings. Sadly, I have since heard quite a few accounts of this by people who use sticks, or have some kind of visible disability. It doesn't make it feel any better though.

Windy's evening lecture

With all of these deeply embedded experiences, I went to Windy's talk. I arrived and was welcomed in. As I listened to him, I wondered if I could use his experience to help me gain a different perspective toward my difficulty. I couldn't change my MS, but perhaps I could change my thinking surrounding it. My feelings felt too overwhelming to deal with. So when he asked if anyone would like to go to the front to have a conversation with him, I put my hand up. Not having done anything like that before, I did not know what to expect, or what was expected of me.

The first thing Windy did was to ask me to turn my chair around. I thought that he meant to the audience, so I turned to face them. Immediately, I had a deep feeling of being 'damaged' in some way, and him rejecting me, so thought that was why he asked me to turn around. But I hadn't realised that he meant to turn toward him. It was the opposite.

Turning my chair back to face Windy, now felt very 'intimate'. It felt important for me to know that he wanted me to be there. When I first started speaking, I thought that I may be overly aware of everyone 'listening in', so thought I might freeze in conversation. However, after a minute or two of settling into my new role of participant, as I listened to Windy's reassuring voice, it was as if the audience faded into the background. It felt like it was just us, being with each other.

It was almost like some kind of light was slowly beginning to come on in my mind as we spoke. I also could not 'hide' or deflect the conversation as Windy's focus of attention was fully on me. I found it challenging, trying to answer questions on the spot, but realised if I had gone away, it would have taken much longer for me to think about things, before coming back to talk again and I may have gone off subject (deliberately, because I wouldn't perhaps want to face things). There was an immediacy about our talking. Windy maintained narrowing his questions down, as we spoke, for him to confirm and understand what I was telling him. And then, suddenly, there it was. Through our conversation, we got to my difficulty. I found it hard for me to admit (to myself) and say out loud, that what I was feeling was in fact shame. I had never considered this before. I immediately tried to deny this thinking "no, that's not right," but then realised, with a growing uncomfortable feeling, that Windy was right. I felt ashamed that I felt shame! Also admitting it, in front of everyone. Windy though had given me a different perspective as to how to begin to change my thinking towards this. After our conversation, I realised I had been very harsh toward myself for a long time. I am grateful that I had the opportunity to speak with Windy that evening, and feel it has changed my awareness as to what has possibly been holding me back.

Notes

1 Due to the inflexibility of the convener of the event, who insisted we leave exactly at the time the event was scheduled to finish, the audience had no time to discuss the conversation. This is an unusual occurrence, but reminds me of the importance of clarifying expectations with respect to time before an event begins.

2 'Spaz' is an abusive short-hand version of 'spastic', which is, in turn, a derogatory term for someone with a disability that involves involuntary movements.

Chapter 13

Working at the base of the pillar: Ulrike

Length of conversation = 31 minutes and 47 seconds

Ulrike attended a day's workshop on 'Working Very Briefly with Clients' that I ran for the Bromley Community Counselling Service (BCCS) on 29 July 2017. The event was advertised as follows:

> In this workshop, I will outline my own approach to working very briefly with clients. By this I mean between 1 and 3 sessions. I will also consider very brief work from a wider perspective and will look at the indications and contraindications of such work. We will then discuss counsellors' views and feelings about working very briefly. The question will be put: Can and should BCCS offer a subsidiary service based on very brief work?
>
> I am very happy to demonstrate my work with volunteers from the audience who want help with a genuine concern or issue, is keen to 'grasp the nettle' and are prepared to discuss this concern or issue in front of the group. Each piece of work will then be discussed. In past workshops, this has been the most valuable part of the session.

Ulrike volunteered to discuss her issue with 'self-hatred' at this workshop.

WINDY: OK, Ulrike, what problem can I help you with this afternoon?
ULRIKE: I suffer from chronic fatigue syndrome, and I've suffered from it for five years. It was triggered by some vaccinations, but since then I have realised that it was a long time in coming. I think the underlying problem is and was that I have always pushed myself a lot, and there is a lot of perfectionism and

that I am never good enough, this thinking. I think, at the very bottom of it is a kind of self-hatred.

WINDY: OK. And you connect these issues with the chronic fatigue?

ULRIKE: Yes.

WINDY: In what way do you connect them?

ULRIKE: Because I always used to go over my limit. I don't think I was even aware of my own physical, emotional, mental limits. When I was, I would still push myself even further and further. Even now, although I have reduced ability – physical, emotional and mental – I still find myself pushing myself harder.

WINDY: And what would you like to achieve from our discussion this afternoon?

ULRIKE: Well, ideally, I'd like to get rid of my self-hatred, but that's probably a tall order. Maybe we can do something with the perfectionism or this feeling of not being good enough?

[I note Ulrike's wish to 'get rid of self-hatred'. My own goal, as yet unexpressed, is to have her work towards something healthy, rather than eliminate something unhealthy.]

WINDY: Do you link the perfectionism and self-hatred?

ULRIKE: Yes.

WINDY: How do you link it?

ULRIKE: …It's all linked together. The perfectionism comes because I feel I'm not good enough.

WINDY: So you aren't good enough is at the base, right?

ULRIKE: Yes, and further down is this self-hatred, which then probably speaks to me, "You're not good enough."

WINDY: OK. So, if you were to put some words to the self-hatred attitude, what would it be?

ULRIKE: …You're a failure. You have no right to exist. You're a bad person.

WINDY: And that then leads to the next layer up, which is you're not good enough?

ULRIKE: Yes, so I need to try harder to be better.

WINDY: So the 'I'm not good enough' leads you to try harder.

ULRIKE: Yes.

WINDY: And what's the effect of the try harder?

ULRIKE: That's the perfectionism, and, obviously, then, because I try harder, even though I've already tried harder over my limit, I exhaust myself, and I never get anywhere because it's in my own mind.

WINDY: So it goes self-hatred – either you're a failure or you have no right to exist or you're a bad person – 'I'm not good enough,' perfectionistic striving, overworking – consequence is exhaustion.

ULRIKE: Yes.

WINDY: So, if we were to construct a different pillar, does that sound like a pillar?

[I argued in the first part of this book that my aim is to assess a specific volunteer-nominated problem, rather than carry out a 'case conceptualisation' of the person's concerns. However, given how Ulrike discusses her concerns as the discussion unfolds, I am carrying out a brief form of such conceptualisation. As Ulrike spoke, I had an image of a pillar with self-hatred at the base and other concerns hierarchically organised upon this base. I used this image to invite her to construct a different pillar. I am hoping that this approach would help us both to set a meaningful, but more concrete goal for Ulrike.

The fact that I will occasionally do some 'case conceptualisation' work in a VBTC, I think, shows the flexibility of my approach.]

ULRIKE: Yes.

WINDY: So what would the new pillar look like?

ULRIKE: Well, the foundation would have to be I can love myself, or maybe even deeper, I am loved, as a very existential...

WINDY: I am loved by whom?

ULRIKE: That's a very good question. Well, historically, obviously it all goes back to my family and my parents, which is probably too long to go into, and we can't redo that, in a way.

WINDY: No.

ULRIKE: Maybe I am loved by God. Although I know that in my head, but the biggest distance is between my head and my heart.

WINDY: So, if you were loved by God and you really felt it, what difference would it make to the next layer up?

ULRIKE: I would feel I don't have to be good enough, because I'm loved unconditionally. It wouldn't depend on what I have to do. I would just be and it would be OK.

WINDY: OK, so, "If I feel that I'm loved unconditionally by God, then it would have an effect on the next layer up," because, instead of "I'm not good enough," you would think what?

ULRIKE: I would think I'm not perfect but I'm loved anyway.

WINDY: "I'm not perfect, but God loves me anyway."

ULRIKE: Yes.

WINDY: OK. And then what would that impact have on your striving?

ULRIKE: It would be the other way round: I would not have to work hard to justify my existence, but my existence would've been justified, and that's why I can be productive.

WINDY: Right, OK.

ULRIKE: It's not that I would push myself, but I would…be inspired – it's not the right word, 'inspired', but it would just flow naturally from being accepted, feeling accepted.

[What I have done here is to help Ulrike construct an alternative pillar with healthy alternatives to unhealthy processes at each of the pillar's layers.]

WINDY: OK, so it sounds like we can intervene at any of these levels.

ULRIKE: Yeah.

WINDY: So, if we took the ambitious approach, we would have a look at this helping you to feel that you were loved by God. Do you want to try some of that?

[Theoretically, helping Ulrike to construct a healthier base would be the more influential in terms of the spread of effect, but also the more ambitious, as I note. Ordinarily, I would invite the person to choose where to intervene in a complex situation, but I had a sense that taking the 'ambitious approach' would be more beneficial for Ulrike and also show the audience what can be achieved in a short time with an issue at the base of a person's concerns.]

ULRIKE: Yeah.

WINDY: Tell me about your relationship with God.

[I begin to assess the problem at the base of the pillar – Ulrike not feeling that she is loved by God.]

ULRIKE: I'm a Christian and so I have a relationship with God the Father, God the Son – Jesus Christ, and the Holy Spirit. The most troublesome is my relationship with God the Father because of my experience with my earthly father, because, as soon as I address God as my father, I see him as my father. All my father issues come into the relationship. So, I want to trust him with my whole heart.

WINDY: Trust whom?

ULRIKE: Trust God the Father, with my whole heart, but it's a real struggle, and sometimes it's better and sometimes I just run away.

WINDY: OK, so what if you did not contaminate God the Father with your real father? What difference would that make?

[From what Ulrike has said, the word 'contamination' seemed to fit, but I wished I had checked this with her and invited her to use her language, rather than to continue to use mine, as we will see.]

ULRIKE: That would be the solution, really, but I find it very difficult to even picture, in my head, what would a good earthly father have looked like.

WINDY: And you need to do that before you're loved by God the Father?

ULRIKE: No, he loves me anyway.

WINDY: I'm sorry, what did you say?

ULRIKE: He loves me anyway.

WINDY: How do you know?

ULRIKE: Because the Bible tells me.

WINDY: It tells you but do you feel it?

ULRIKE: That's what I am trying to say. He loves me anyway, but, if I don't feel it, it doesn't make any difference.

WINDY: So what conditions would have to exist for you to feel it?

ULRIKE: …I don't know…Sometimes I do feel it.

WINDY: You do feel it.

ULRIKE: Sometimes.

WINDY: Tell me about those times.

[If a volunteer has already done what they want to do, my aim is to find out more about this and build on it, if relevant. I am influenced in this respect by solution-focused therapists (Ratner, George & Iveson, 2012).]

ULRIKE: I can never really tell what it was, but, somehow, suddenly opens this door and all this rubbish, so to speak, from my earthly father falls to the wayside, and suddenly I'm there and I feel like I can sit on God the Father's lap, and I feel loved. But that is almost like fireworks.

WINDY: OK, so it sounds like, to me, and you correct me if I'm wrong, I want to understand this, that the times when you feel loved by God are times when there's no contamination between God the Father and your real father.

ULRIKE: Yes.

WINDY: As you say it falls away.

ULRIKE: Yeah.

WINDY: Now is it possible for you to feel loved by God if you still have those contaminating thoughts in terms of how your father treated you? Is it possible for you to feel loved by God under those conditions?

[There are times in a conversation where I have a choice of direction. This is one of those times. I could have chosen to discover what Ulrike does to lead the 'rubbish from her earthly father to fall to the wayside'. What I chose to do is to go a different route. Rather than help her to 'decontaminate' her mind, I want to help her to deal with the contamination. This is in keeping with the adversity-focused nature of my work that distinguishes it from solution-focused work. I want to help her both to deal with the adversity and then pursue a solution. My view is that the latter is enhanced by the former.]

ULRIKE: Yes, but, as you said, you used the word 'contaminated', it is smudged. It is a blurry picture.

WINDY: Who's in charge of un-munching it and un-blurring it?

[This is curious. Ulrike clearly uses the word 'smudged', but I think she said 'munched', so I use what I think she said rather than what she actually said. Interestingly, she says in her response above, "you used the word 'contaminated'." This shows that while she understood it, she did not resonate with it and goes on to use her own words 'smudged' and 'blurry'. I get the latter right but, sadly, not the former. All this shows, I believe, the importance of using words with which the volunteer resonates.]

ULRIKE: Moi.

WINDY: Yes, you. So, if you were to do the un-blurring, un-munching, how would you do that?

ULRIKE: …

WINDY: So the reality is that you're still going to have those thoughts, right?

ULRIKE: Yes.

WINDY: In terms of your real father.

ULRIKE: Yes.

WINDY: So the thoughts are there, right?

ULRIKE: Yeah.

WINDY: And your choice is to blur and munch or un-blur and un-munch, without getting rid of this.

ULRIKE: …How do you mean 'without getting rid of this'?

WINDY: It exists.

ULRIKE: OK, yes, because the past is the past.

WINDY: And what we know about thoughts, the more you try to get rid of thoughts, what happens?

ULRIKE: Yes, the elephant.

WINDY: The elephant, exactly.

ULRIKE: Don't think of the elephant, yeah.

[This shows me that Ulrike understands the paradoxical effects of trying to get rid of thoughts. If you hold in your mind the thought or image of an elephant and try to eliminate that thought or image, paradoxically the reverse happens. You will think of it more. This opens the way for me to help her deal with her negative thoughts about her earthly father in a different way, as we will see.]

WINDY: So there you are, there's God the Father waiting for you to sit on his lap, here's the thoughts about your real father, here's your choice between munching and blurring, and un-munching and un-blurring, right?

ULRIKE: Yeah.

WINDY: It's easy for you to munch and blur.

ULRIKE: Absolutely.

WINDY: I don't have to teach you about that.

ULRIKE: It comes automatically.

WINDY: But you can tell me how do you munch and blur? You've got the thoughts about your real father, tell me how you munch and blur?

[Using the concepts of 'munch' and 'blur', which should, of course, be 'smudge' and 'blur', I want to find out more about how the thoughts about her real father prevent her from feeling rather than knowing that she is loved by God the Father.]

ULRIKE: It happens without even consciously doing anything. It's just there.

WINDY: No.

ULRIKE: It's negating the good things that I know about God the Father.

WINDY: OK, so what does that sound like? What form do those negating thoughts take?

ULRIKE: It sort of disputes what I know about God.

WINDY: Tell me.

ULRIKE: For example, thoughts like, "Yes, I can read you are kind." I'm talking to God.

WINDY: No, don't talk to God yet.

ULRIKE: Not yet? OK.

WINDY: We'll get to God in a minute. It's your thoughts about your father.

[Here, I quickly intervene to keep the focus on the problem – how Ulrike's negative thoughts about her earthly father interfere with her feeling loved by the heavenly father. In retrospect, I could have asked for a specific example, but Ulrike soon provides me with the concrete information I need to help her, as we will see.]

ULRIKE: OK.

WINDY: What's the blurring and munching thoughts that you have about your father, because that's what happens, right? You relate to God, these thoughts about your father come up, you blur and munch them, and you can't get to God.

ULRIKE: Yep.

WINDY: So I want to clear away the pathway so that you can get to God.

ULRIKE: So the thoughts are, "You're not reliable, you're dangerous."

WINDY: When you say that, whose thoughts are they?

ULRIKE: My thoughts about my earthly father.

WINDY: OK, right.

ULRIKE: So, "You're not reliable, you're dangerous, you stab a knife in my back when I least expect it, when I just think our relationship is fine and going to work…You are a drunk. You're emotionally unstable and you can't give me stability."

[At the time, I am treating these as inferences (at 'A'). Note that I make no attempt to question their accuracy.]

WINDY: What's the feelings that you have when you have those thoughts?

*[Having gotten 'A' – or more accurately several 'A's – which, as you will
see, I lump together to form a collective 'A', I ask for her emotional 'C'.]*

ULRIKE: I'm close to tears.

*[Ulrike's emotional response is important for a number of reasons. It
shows me that I am on an important track and it demonstrates that she
is emotionally engaged with a meaningful issue.]*

WINDY: With what feeling?

ULRIKE: Sadness and anger.

WINDY: Which of those two emotions is going to stop you from
getting closer to God?

*[In asking this question, I am mindful of Ulrike's goal of feeling loved
by God. I want to discover the major obstacle to this goal, which will
then become the target problem. Note that we are at the midpoint of
the conversation. It has taken me a long time to get to this point, but
as I said in the first part of the book, it is important to understand the
context of the person's main issue and to give due credit to the complexity of the problem the person brings. It is also important for me to
show that I understand Ulrike's concerns from her frame of reference.
I would argue that this has been time very well spent and enables me to
help Ulrike in a more meaningful way than if I had edited out the complexity and focused very early on a specific problem.]*

ULRIKE: Anger.

WINDY: OK, now let's have a look at your anger there, OK?

ULRIKE: Yep.

WINDY: Now…there are two types of anger, as far as I can tell, and
they both have a common root, and that is they're both based on
the idea that you really don't like what your father's done.

*[Having made the point above that the time I have spent understanding
the complexity of Ulrike's problem has been time well spent, I am
aware of the passage of time and make a deliberate decision to be
theory driven in outlining my views on anger. I wish, however, that
I had asked her permission to do this rather than going ahead and
doing it.]*

ULRIKE: Yeah.

WINDY: He's stabbed you in the back, he's been unreliable, he's done this, that and the other, and you're going to be angry about that. The question is what type of anger is it? Is it the kind of anger that is based on the philosophy, 'and you shouldn't be like that, you should be more like God the Father' or 'well, sadly and unfortunately, you don't have to be the kind of father that I want you to be'? When you're really angry, what kind of idea underpins that?

[As discussed in Chapter 6, unhealthy anger is based on a rigid attitude and healthy anger is based on a flexible attitude. I am using this attitudinal approach to help Ulrike to determine whether her anger is healthy or unhealthy. I wished I had used the term 'must' instead of 'should' or used the qualifier 'absolutely' when using the word 'should'.]

ULRIKE: The second thing that you've just described isn't anger, is it, to say, 'sadly, you weren't the father'?
WINDY: It is, because you still don't like what your father did to you.
ULRIKE: OK. It's the first one.
WINDY: What would happen if you really believed the second?

[Having established that Ulrike's anger is unhealthy and based on a rigid attitude, I quickly ask what would be the consequence of believing the flexible attitude.]

ULRIKE: I could let go.
WINDY: Right. And the pathway to meet God is what? Cleared or still blocked?
ULRIKE: It would be a lot more cleared, I think.

[Ulrike shows that she can see the link between the flexible attitude and her goal of becoming closer to God the Father.]

WINDY: OK. So now the question is, now we're talking about your relationship in terms of your attitude towards your real father. Is he still alive, by the way?
ULRIKE: No.
WINDY: So he acted in all kinds of ways that were very negative for you.

[This is the collective 'A'. I am not focusing on any one of her father's behaviours, because Ulrike talks about them collectively.]

ULRIKE: Yes.

WINDY: No doubt about that. And we know that you really wished that he hadn't have done that, right?

[Here I am reiterating that I am assuming that 'A' is correct and I am stressing that she has a strong desire that is present in both her rigid attitude and her flexible attitude.]

ULRIKE: Yeah. I'm welling up again.

[Ulrike is still emotionally engaged and showing that this is an important issue for her.]

WINDY: OK, that's fine. Now the question is, Ulrike, and this is the difficult bit, when you were growing up, were you asked to take cod liver oil?

[I am alerting her to the idea that I will be asking her to swallow what I call one of 'life's bitter pills'. In her case, no matter how important it was and is to her that her father was different, sadly and regrettably, he did not have to be the father she wanted him to be.]

ULRIKE: Yes.

WINDY: And you know the principle of the cod liver oil?

ULRIKE: No.

WINDY: It didn't taste nice but it was good for you.

ULRIKE: Yes.

WINDY: So I'm going to invite you to maybe take some psychological cod liver oil. Are you willing to look at it?

ULRIKE: Yes.

WINDY: The question is did your father have to be the way you wanted him to be or not?

ULRIKE: No, he didn't have to be.

WINDY: OK. Now, if you really focused on that and you focused on the idea that he really acted badly towards you in all kinds of ways, but, sadly and regretfully, he didn't have to be the father that you wanted him to be, but there's a sadness in having that loss of not having the father that you wanted. So, you've got the anger that he treated you badly, you're not demanding that he had to be the way you wanted him to be and there's a sadness about the fact that he wasn't.

[Having helped her to see that she could feel healthily angry about her father's behaviour, I reiterate that when she focuses on the inference of loss, then she will feel sad.]

ULRIKE: Yes.

WINDY: If you put all those together and you really digested that, and allowed the cod liver oil to digest through your body, would the pathway to the real God be clearer for you?

[Here, I keep reiterating the link between healthy attitudes and her goal of feeling loved by God the Father.]

ULRIKE: Yeah, I think so.

WINDY: OK. Now, why don't you put, in your own words, what I'm offering you, to see if I've made myself clear?

[We have covered a lot of ground and I want to ensure that I have made myself understood, so I ask Ulrike to summarise what we have discussed.]

ULRIKE: That, if I managed to digest the fact that my father…didn't have to be the father I wanted him to be, and if I came to terms with the sadness and the anger that goes with that…

WINDY: Without getting rid of it. The anger: he acted badly towards you; and the loss: you didn't have the father that you wanted.

ULRIKE: Yeah, OK. That's important. Without getting rid of the anger and the sadness.

WINDY: Right. All you're getting rid of is the unhealthy anger; the demandingness, "He shouldn't have treated me this way."

ULRIKE: Yes, OK. So, if I could let go or digest the unhealthy anger, then I would, at least what I can sense, at the moment, I think I would feel a lot freer towards God the Father.

WINDY: OK. Now can you feel any resistance in yourself towards doing that?

[Ulrike is accurate in her summary so I move on to seeing if she has any DROs to implementing it.]

ULRIKE: Yes, and I think it's because I'm so used to this old pattern.

WINDY: OK. So, the resistance is you'll experience unfamiliarity.

ULRIKE: Yes, and also, there is a fear that it might not work.

WINDY: OK, so, if you tolerated the unfamiliarity. You say, "I don't usually do this, but I'm going to do this with unfamiliarity," would that make a difference, if you tolerated the unfamiliarity?

ULRIKE: …

WINDY: Or do you need the familiarity of what you usually do?

ULRIKE: I can feel that the pull is very strong, of this familiarity, but I also recognise that, without overcoming that, I won't be able to let it go.

WINDY: Yeah. Just stand that at the side for a minute. Let's suppose that somebody rang your doorbell, and you answered it and there was nobody there. So, they rang once. And then they rang twice, and you opened up and nobody. And you were used to going to the door every time the doorbell rang. So, at what point would you not go and answer the door?

ULRIKE: After the second time or third.

WINDY: Or even longer, but it would be unfamiliar. You would have to go against your familiar tendency to open up the door.

ULRIKE: Yes.

WINDY: So what I'm saying to you is, your familiar idea is to jump to, "My father was bad, and he shouldn't have been like that," that's familiar, right?

ULRIKE: Yes.

WINDY: You say, "OK, I've started off like that, but I don't have to continue."

ULRIKE: Yeah.

[My major intervention is to help Ulrike understand that her familiar response can be divided into an action tendency and an overt behaviour and that, while the former is familiar, she does not have to act on it.]

WINDY: Have you ever watched *Mastermind*?

ULRIKE: I don't remember.

WINDY: There was a guy on that called Magnus Magnusson, and his phrase was, "I've started so I'll finish." Have you heard that?

ULRIKE: No.

WINDY: So yours is, "I've started, but I don't have to finish it." "I've started the familiar pattern, but I can interrupt it. I have the choice to interrupt it."

ULRIKE: Yes.

[Because Ulrike had not watched Mastermind, *she doesn't resonate with the catchphrase. In retrospect, I would have been wise to drop it once she had indicated this, thus demonstrating that once I had introduced the topic, I did not have to finish it myself!]*

WINDY: Now the other obstacle you said was what? There's the familiarity and, 'I don't know if it will work'?

ULRIKE: Yes.

WINDY: So, if I gave you a guarantee that it would work, would you do it?

ULRIKE: Yes.

WINDY: OK, so what you're demanding is a guarantee, isn't it?

ULRIKE: Yeah, but I also realise, if it doesn't work, I'm not any worse off than I am now.

WINDY: That's right. So why don't you do it without the guarantee?

ULRIKE: That's a deal.

[Ulrike seems more open to the idea of going forward without the guarantee that it will work.]

WINDY: OK, so...[Pause] Let's see if we can practise that.

[At this point, I want to give Ulrike an opportunity to practise her flexible attitude in an emotionally impactful way. I do this by encouraging her to engage in some chairwork (Kellogg, 2015). I could have set this up better, giving a rationale and asking for her permission to participate. I thought about doing so at the time, but my sense was that we both would have lost the impetus that we had. You will see that I am quite directive in chairwork. I do this to help Ulrike to get the most out of what emerges in the process.]

ULRIKE: OK.

WINDY: So you sit over here and be the Ulrike, whose first response is to be demanding about your father, and then we'll get you to respond to that, shall we?

ULRIKE: OK.

WINDY: Come here and we'll have a typical scenario that the thought about your father starts about his unreliability?

ULRIKE: Yes.

WINDY: OK, so tell Ulrike that your father was unreliable and he shouldn't have been that way. Just kind of say that to her.

ULRIKE: OK, so Ulrike's sitting there.

WINDY: Yeah.

ULRIKE: OK.

WINDY: You're Ulrike and she's Ulrike. You're the Ulrike that is used to driving the familiar pattern: "My father shouldn't..."

ULRIKE: Yes. You know he should not have been a drunk. He should have cared better for his family. He should have been there for you. He should not have been abusive. He should not have been unreliable in his emotional dealings with you.

WINDY: OK. So, what are you going to say to 'Ulrike, the Should'?

ULRIKE: You know, yep, you're absolutely right, he should not have, but he wasn't, and that was maybe not even his choice, maybe that was because of his upbringing. He just wasn't the father that you needed, and that's hard.

WINDY: OK, and I'm just going to add a little bit and say, "And, ideally, he shouldn't have been the way he was, but, in reality, he should be the way he was because he was. That's the way he was, and my father had to be my father because of what was going on inside his head, but, ideally, he shouldn't have been that way." So, say that.

ULRIKE: OK. Ideally, he should not have been the way he was, but he should have been the way he was, because he was your father, and that's how he was.

WINDY: But his behaviour was pretty lousy.

ULRIKE: But his behaviour was pretty lousy.

WINDY: OK, let's see what she says about that.

ULRIKE: I'm trying to digest this all because it's...[Pause] Yes, it's right. On the one hand, he should not have been like this; he didn't represent good fatherhood, but, on the other hand, yes, it's true, that's who he was and he still was my father.

WINDY: And I can acknowledge that and have a clearer path towards God the Father.

ULRIKE: And I can acknowledge that and have a clearer path towards God the Father.

WINDY: Even though I have negative thoughts about how my father behaved.

ULRIKE: Even though I have negative thoughts about how my father behaved.

WINDY: Let's see what she says.

ULRIKE: You know what, it can't be that easy. That sounds too easy. Is that all it is?

WINDY: I've got to really suffer first before I digest this.

ULRIKE: (Laughter) That fits. You hit the nail on the head.

[This really strikes a chord with Ulrike, but I leave it because it would have taken us away from the focus we had created and maintained at this point of the process.]

WINDY: OK, sit down and we'll stop there.

ULRIKE: Thank you.

WINDY: You see, you're not making any distinction between simple and easy. It's simple but it's not easy. And the work that you need to do is to recognise that you are in a familiar pattern. You're going to start off with two things about your father: one is how he failed you, which we're not arguing about; and (b) he shouldn't have done that, because that's not what fathers do. Fathers have to be…Did he go to a training school for fathers?

ULRIKE: Is there one?

WINDY: I don't know.

ULRIKE: That's the problem.

WINDY: So, the problem is, even if there was one, I'm not sure he would've been a good student. You see, you can have those negative thoughts about your father and have a clearer pathway to God, if you allow yourself the choice to recognise and accept, but not like, the father that you had, and that, sadly and regretfully, he doesn't have to be the father that you've always wanted, and that's sad. If you practise that, how could God help you do that practice?

ULRIKE: [Pause] I feel like I have to put in all the work, really.

WINDY: You mean God doesn't have to do all the work?

ULRIKE: No, but that's what I'm feeling that I have to do it. Actually, he has already done it.

WINDY: In what way?

ULRIKE: By telling me, in the Bible, about his love, and by sending his son to die for me. That was his biggest sacrifice.

WINDY: OK, so you've got your bit to do and God's got his bit to do. He's already done his bit, but you need to remind yourself of that, because it's not only down to you; it's a joint effort. So maybe you also need to have a conversation with God on the point of, "We're in this together – you're helping me towards my way back to you to get this unconditional love, and I'm helping myself towards that as well. You're shining the light, and I'm doing my bit as well."

[I say this to move Ulrike away from the idea that she has to do all the work by herself. I am trying to form a working alliance between her and God.]

ULRIKE: Yeah.

WINDY: How does that feel?

ULRIKE: That makes a lot of sense.

WINDY: Yeah?

ULRIKE: Yeah.

WINDY: OK. So why don't you summarise the work that we've done so far?

[Again, I ask Ulrike to summarise as I sense that the conversation will soon be coming to a close.]

ULRIKE: Well…the problem we were working at was this self-hatred, and the…consequences that build up like a pillar of trying to be a better person and not feeling good enough. You asked what would it look like if there was another pillar that was healthy and what would the basis be. So that's how we came about to talk about the God stuff.

WINDY: Yes, that's where we chose to do that work, isn't it?

ULRIKE: Yeah.…So…sorry, I find it really difficult to concentrate.

WINDY: That's OK.

ULRIKE: [Pause] You said to me that there are two types of anger: there's this type of anger that says my father should have been a better father.

WINDY: In an absolute way.

ULRIKE: In an absolute way.

WINDY: Not ideally.

ULRIKE: Yeah. And that's the bit that keeps me tied to the wrong father image, so to speak to.

WINDY: That's good.

ULRIKE: Yeah, and that's why I can't let go.

WINDY: Right.

ULRIKE: And, as I understand, I need to digest that.

WINDY: What would be a physical representation of letting go when you're in that situation?

ULRIKE: Yeah, I would have to release [clenches and then unclenches both fists and moves arms apart].

WINDY: OK. That's one of the things you can do to break the pattern, to recognise that, when you're, initially, doing that [clenches fists], you can go [unclenches fists and moves arms apart], "Oh, wait a minute, I can release that and remind myself that my father, sadly, didn't have to be the way I wanted him to be, and that would be a pathway back to God the Father."

ULRIKE: Yeah, OK. So physically doing it.

WINDY: Yeah.

ULRIKE: OK.

WINDY: It would be a reminder for you.

ULRIKE: Yes.

[As Ulrike made a physical representation of change with her hands and arms, I use this same gesture to reinforce the change that she has made and that she can utilise these gestures to accompany and underscore the change that she needs to make.]

WINDY: OK. And then we talked about the fact that it's too easy.

ULRIKE: Yeah, it really made me laugh what you said: "You really need to suffer, don't you?" because that's typical, I think, of this self-hatred.

WINDY: Yeah.

ULRIKE: In my life there is almost like an unwritten law: my life has to be difficult. That's the way I see my life.

[This seems to be an important core attitude for Ulrike. Unfortunately, we don't have any time to do any work on this attitude, and to do so at this point would detract from what I hope she will be taking away from our conversation.]

WINDY: Right, but, if you recognised that what you need to do is, gently, just do the work when it comes up, you don't have to overwork it, because that's also a sign of self-hatred.

ULRIKE: Yeah.

WINDY: And, just leave you with one thing, when you find yourself in the familiar patterns of the overwork and the 'I'm not good enough', go to the base, touch base with your attitude towards your father, get practise of letting that go, because that's where you need to go; you need to go to the base to do the work.

[I remind her of the importance of going to the base of the pillar when she recognises unhelpful familiar patterns higher up.]

ULRIKE: Yeah, great.

WINDY: How do you feel about that?

ULRIKE: It sounds very exciting.

WINDY: Good. I wish you well.

Follow-up

Three months later, in response to my request for her experiences of our conversation, Ulrike wrote the following:

"This is a bad joke!" I thought cynically when I read the flyer at the counselling agency that I was volunteering with, announcing a [continuing professional development] day with Windy Dryden on very brief therapy (1–3 sessions). How could anybody have the 'cheek' to offer therapy that would solve ANYTHING in one to three sessions, when my own experience of counselling and psychotherapy was that it had taken me decades of on and off therapy to help me deal with my issues and, when all I had learned as a counsellor myself so far was that it took weeks of therapy to even just establish a good therapeutic relationship?

I did not really know much about CBT let alone REBT. I had only qualified the year before and had never researched CBT in any depth. The little that I had come across (not necessarily in my training) seemed rather superficial to me, and I thought it was doctoring the symptoms but ignoring the potentially deep-rooted causes. Yes, I had a bone or two to pick with CBT! How did they dare to offer quick solutions when my own experience of therapy with sustainable results stretched to decades of treatment?!

But despite the little that I did and do know, I knew that Windy Dryden was THE authority on the subject, so I decided to 'come along' to the CPD day, looking forward to the hash he would make of it…

Am I glad I 'came along'! As Windy was speaking I had to admit that what he was saying was making a lot of sense, particularly when he specified the indications (and limitations) for very brief therapy. So, he was NOT suggesting that issues that had taken me decades to grapple with could have been sorted with less than a handful of sessions! What a relief!

And then my ears pricked up when he said something about CBT that so echoed my own rather cynical thoughts. He said something about a general misunderstanding that CBT was about positive thinking, ignoring what he called the 'Dryden's daily dose of discomfort' we should all be prepared to accept and welcome in our lives. That was a revelation and a clincher for me! I had often felt CBT was just sugar-coating the difficulties we can have in life, yet here was the 'CBT pope' advocating a different view. And the discomfort popped up again in my demo session with Windy later on, where it really struck me as very relevant to my dealing with my issues.

I was very pleased when he accepted me as one of the volunteers for his demo sessions that day. He had 'warned' me that he would be interrupting me frequently (if gently) which was one of the main differences to the type of therapy I had both experienced and provided up to that point, but I got used to it quickly. His questions were very sharp, guiding me to the crucial issues regarding my topic, and we quickly started to 'delve deep'.

There was a point where I hesitated with my answer, when he asked me who I needed to feel loved by in order to let go of striving for perfectionism. Immediately I thought "by God," but I was not sure I could give an answer like that in a public session. But then I decided on the spur of the moment to be as honest as possible and gave just that as reply. From there the session took an entirely unexpected turn.

Only after listening to the recorded session Windy made available to me afterwards did I realise that we might have misunderstood each other due to me not being explicit enough. I have been so used to battling with the issue of a distorted father image and hence image of God the Father that I had not pointed out that the transference from my biological father to my divine Father was not a conscious process. I believe we may have talked cross purposes there, leading Windy to assume every time I addressed my heavenly Dad I was thinking of my biological father. This is not the case. It is a subconscious process. My father image in general has just been so twisted by my biological father that any idea of fatherhood is tainted because of it. Nevertheless, I do not think this made any of the session less valuable for me.

It was an eye opener when Windy talked about the two different types of anger and that it was important to let go of the unhealthy type but important to have the healthy type of anger (the one which did not seem to be anger to me in the first place). When we talked about releasing my expectations of my biological father and Windy encouraged me to make this accompanying movement with my hands every time I wanted to let go of my anger against my father, I felt something happening deep inside me. At the moment of opening my hands and arms in this gesture of releasing, something very real but invisible happened to me. It is difficult to describe, but I believe it was a true letting go experience, although I did not communicate that at the time.

Looking back, the part about releasing/letting go was about forgiveness, but I am so glad Windy never mentioned this word. I have done a lot of forgiveness over the years, but a lot of the time it was a decision taken with my intellect, but my emotions still could not follow. The way Windy was talking to me reached the emotional level so that the releasing was done on that level, too, which is what I experienced so powerfully.

I was so keen to work with the recording and transcription that Windy so kindly was going to send me from my session with him, but sadly only two days after our encounter something happened that took my focus completely off it: my beloved little cat was diagnosed with a very aggressive form of cancer and within less than a fortnight had to be put to sleep. Since I was living alone and she was my life companion, this was a major bereavement for me and I grieved terribly for her, even before she was gone and up to long afterwards. My plans to work with this valuable material and the momentum the session with Windy had given me were, unfortunately, lost in the process of grieving.

Nevertheless, the 'father-topic' that had been on my agenda for decades was coming more and more into focus. In my own personal therapy I had started receiving [eye movement desensitisation and reprogramming] and we worked through a situation where my father had threatened to kill my little brother, my mother and me when I was still very young. This addressed a lot of the fear that I have been living with ever since and together with Windy's session, which dealt with the anger and sadness about my father, will continue to have a big positive effect on my relationship with God my heavenly Dad and with myself. The future will show just how big.

Chapter 14

"Keep alive, keep young and stay free!": Carla

Length of conversation = 12 minutes and 2 seconds

Carla is a helping professional who attended a one-day workshop that I gave on single-session and very brief interventions in Campinas, Brazil, on 23 July 2016. During the workshop, I was discussing how to help people deal with their development-based objectives most often associated with coaching. I offered to demonstrate how I work with such issues and Carla volunteered. Her development-based objective was related to health and exercise. Later, she gave me permission to include our interview in this book with commentary and provided a short email follow-up report 14 months after our conversation, which I reproduce at the end of the chapter.

WINDY: OK, Carla, if, at the end of our session, you would have achieved what you wanted to achieve in coming up here, what would that be?

[Right from the start, I take an objective-focused approach, which is typical in a very brief coaching contract where the emphasis is on furthering the person's development.]

CARLA: To exercise every day, at least five times a week.

WINDY: Let's be clear: so your goal is to do exercises between five and seven days a week?

CARLA: Yeah, this is my doctor's advice.

WINDY: And what do you think of that advice?

[Here, I want to be sure Carla is committed to the objective even though it was advised by her doctor.]

CARLA: I had my check-up last year, and she advised me to start doing exercises again. I did it before, more than a decade ago, and I just lost track and I started to join...

WINDY: So you lost the track, did you say?

CARLA: To do every day exercises. Then at the end of the year, I started this year without exercise. So, I know I must do this, but I don't know why I can't.

WINDY: Do you want to do the exercises?

[Again, I want to clarify if this is an intrinsic or extrinsic objective of Carla's.]

CARLA: Yes, I want to, because I know it will help me. More than ten years ago I was diagnosed with diabetes, and I was an obese person, and I did everything to change it. So, I'm OK now, and my goal is to keep my cholesterol level below 90.

WINDY: So your goal is to keep your cholesterol level below a certain level, and you have been advised to do these exercises.

CARLA: Yeah.

WINDY: And you agree with your doctor that it's a good idea.

CARLA: Yeah, because I work with eating disorders, and I know that obesity and diabetes and no exercise and bad food choices are against your health. I know all this.

WINDY: So, before we go into things, do you have any doubts, reservations and objections to your doctor's advice?

CARLA: No. I trust her.

WINDY: So when do you want to do these exercises? Let's be clear. When in the day do you want to do them?

[Having established that this is an intrinsic objective, I encourage Carla to set specific referents for the objective that is to carry out physical exercises. I do this also to establish whether or not Carla can integrate these exercises into her life, which is an important consideration if Carla is going to maintain any changes she might initially make.]

CARLA: I do prefer to do it in the morning because at night I always have an excuse not to do this. I know that it's much better for me to do it early in the morning.

WINDY: What time?

CARLA: That's the main problem, because nowadays I wake up at 6, leave my house at 7, and start work at 8. That's why I'm doing exercise only on weekends.

WINDY: So you wake up at 6, you leave the house at 7, and you start work at 8?

CARLA: Usually.

WINDY: Who do you work for?

CARLA: For myself.

WINDY: Do you have an understanding boss?

[Since Carla works for herself, I wanted to introduce her to the idea that there is a part of her that is the boss and a part of her that is an employee. Note that her next response indicates that my question caught her by surprise. In my view, such surprise is productive because it helps the coachee begin to look at things differently.]

CARLA: I don't have a boss.

WINDY: You do. You.

CARLA: Oh yes.

WINDY: It's you. Do you have an understanding boss?

CARLA: Yeah.

WINDY: And what hours does your boss ask you to work?

CARLA: Eight hours a day, at least.

WINDY: So that involves you starting work at?

CARLA: 8.

WINDY: And, so, that involves you finishing work at what time?

CARLA: 8, because I have a break for lunch.

WINDY: So you start work at 8 and you finish at 8, so that's 12 hours.

CARLA: Yeah, I have a break.

WINDY: You have a four-hour break for lunch.

CARLA: Two hours – one lunch in the morning for one hour, one at lunchtime.

WINDY: You have two lunchbreaks. So you start at 8.

CARLA: Let me think about this. One choice, if I start at 9.

WINDY: I'm just trying to do the maths.

CARLA: It's a little bit confused, now I'm talking to you.

WINDY: Exactly, so let's be clear. Clarity is an important ingredient. So you start at 8 and you finish at 8.

CARLA: Only two days a week.

WINDY: So you start at 8 and finish at 8, that's 12 hours, minus two hours for lunch, that's 10 hours.

CARLA: Only two days a week.

WINDY: And the rest of the week you do what?

CARLA: Maybe I do the same at home, at the hospital.

WINDY: So who do you work for at the hospital?

CARLA: I'm a volunteer at a psychiatric institute.

WINDY: So, being a volunteer, who's in charge of what time you start?

CARLA: No one.

WINDY: This is interesting, isn't it? So you tell me, "I can't do it in the evening because I find an excuse. In the morning, I get up at 6, 7 and 8," and I say, "Your boss must be terrible," "No, I'm the boss," and then we have to account for the two missing hours and the voluntary. Who's making you do it? Nobody's making you do it. So, what I'm saying is, theoretically, who's in charge of your life?

CARLA: Yeah, maybe I must fire my boss.

WINDY: No. Have a word with your boss.

[Although we are both a little confused concerning Carla's actual work hours, we both agree that Carla is in charge of her life. Her immediate response is to fire her boss, but my response to that is that, instead, 'Carla the employee' needs to have a dialogue with 'Carla the boss'.]

CARLA: I've never thought about this. It's so funny. Just say this again, just in a few minutes, it's wonderful.

[My suggestion seems to have had an emotional impact on Carla.]

WINDY: So what are you going to say to your boss?

CARLA: Be more compassionate.

WINDY: Let's have a dialogue between you and your boss. I'll stand out the way. What's your boss's name?

[In order to promote this dialogue and maintain the emotional impact factor, I suggest that Carla engages in in-session chairwork (Kellogg, 2015).]

CARLA: Carla.

WINDY: So shall we call her Carla Boss, and you're Carla?

CARLA: Ex-obese Carla.

WINDY: Ex-obese Carla and Carla the Boss. OK, so you want the boss to be more compassionate.

CARLA: Yeah.

WINDY: Just stay there. This is Carla the Boss. Tell Carla the Boss that you want her to be more compassionate to you, and explain why.

CARLA: So, Carla Boss, I want you to be more compassionate with me, and maybe you try to do many obligations and many things in your day, and save one hour for exercise.

WINDY: And tell her when you want to do that one hour of exercise.

CARLA: It must be clear, Carla Boss, that I want to do this early in the morning.

WINDY: Tell her what time you want to do it.

CARLA: At 6, not at 5. At 6 will be OK.

WINDY: So, between 6 and 7 you want to do the exercise. Tell her what time you want to start work.

CARLA: Carla Boss, I want to start work at 9.

WINDY: So you want her to be more compassionate towards you and you want her agreement that you can start work at 9. Let's see what she says. Change chairs.

CARLA: Ex-obese Carla, I want you to become healthy, and I do agree that you need to do exercises early in the morning. So it's fine for you to save one hour in the morning, and start work at 9.

WINDY: Let's see what she says.

CARLA: Carla Boss, I want to thank you, because you feel so compassionate about my commitment to be healthy, and not have diabetes again. So I thank you that you agree.

WINDY: Do you want to suggest that you make that agreement a handshake that means something?

CARLA: If you shake hands?

WINDY: Yeah.

CARLA: I wish you to shake hands with me to make this agreement.

WINDY: Let's see what she says.

CARLA: OK, do you want me to shake hands with you? I agree.

WINDY: Stand up a bit. How are we going to do this handshake? For you, what's going to be meaningful? This and this? So I want you to remember this. Can somebody take a picture of this, please?

CARLA: It's a strange gesture, but fine. It feels right.

[I suggested that someone take a photo of this physical expression of their agreement so that she can use this as a vivid reminder of the outcome of the session.]

WINDY: So, what I want you to do is for you to send that picture to her so that she can have a reminder. So, have we solved your problem, do you think?

CARLA: I feel so nice now. I think my head and shoulders are light again. I feel so invigorated, it's incredible.

WINDY: So when are you going to start this routine?

[I asked this question because I wanted Carla to capitalise on the work she had done as soon as possible.]

CARLA: Tomorrow morning.

Follow-up

Three months later, Carla reported that she had maintained the gains that she had implemented after the session.

Fourteen months after the end of the session, Carla sent me the following email in response to my request to include our conversation in this book:

> It's more than one year since that roleplay at FBTC, and the experience changed me in a very special way.
>
> I did realise that the way I was working was too much…and yesterday, for example, I had a lovely 2 hours lunch with my dear friend, talking and laughing, enjoying life and friendship…It's winter time in Brazil, and it's very hard to wake up early under 8°C…and I start going to work by tube, instead of using my car…walking about 40 minutes per day (morning and evening) and not using the escalators anymore!
>
> More than that, I'm sleeping about 7–8 hours per night, instead of 5–6…
>
> I changed my diet (vegetarian) and I feel so much better nowadays.
>
> My lesson from you? Keep alive, keep young and stay free!
>
> I'm going to the last year of my master degree, writing my dissertation, working with love and passion, focused on my health, friends and family, and my love to psychology!
>
> I'm going to be 60 (December 1st) and I'm feeling so good!
>
> *Abraços* from your big fan in Brazil!!!

Afterword

Before bringing the book to a close, I thought that I would make a few observations about my work and its applicability. Given its brief nature and the fact that it intends to give the person something of value to take away and use in their everyday life, it seems to me that this work fits well within the walk-in/drop-in therapeutic services discussed in Hoyt and Talmon (2014a). If structured properly, these services could be offered to people at the point of need and give people something of therapeutic value rather than being placed on a long waiting list of being submitted to a lengthy period of assessment. At the moment, walk-in services are not a feature of the National Health Service (NHS) in Britain, but with some imaginative planning, it could be placed alongside existing services.

Need for research

I have mentioned several times in this book that much of the time I know nothing about the volunteers before I meet them and, in most cases, I do not hear from them again. While this is in keeping with the concept of VBTCs discussed here, this won't do if, for example, the NHS were to consider adopting something akin to this way of working within the context of a delivery system based on walk-in therapeutic services. Here are some research-based questions that need to be answered about VBTCs as currently practised:

- What distinguishes volunteers from non-volunteers?
- What distinguishes volunteers who benefit from VBCTs from those who do not?
- What is it to have been 'helped' in VBCTs? How can this 'benefit' be measured/quantified?

- Are volunteers more or less likely to seek help for the issue that they raised in VBTCs than if they had not raised it?
- To what extent do the pre-VBCT and post-VBCT discussions influence any 'benefits' obtained (understanding the VBCT in the context of live demonstrations)?
- What is the effect of reading (and re-reading) the transcript of the session?
- What is the effect of listening to (and re-listening to) the digital voice recording of the session?
- What are the impacts of the choices that I often offer volunteers in the course of VBCTs?
- What is the impact of humour on the effectiveness of VBTCs?

What is helpful about VBCTs?

If VBTCs are helpful to people, then we need to find out why. My view is that different features of the VBCT process are likely to be helpful for different volunteers. Let me review some possible helpful ingredients.

Relationship factors

These factors are related to the bond domain of the working alliance discussed in Chapter 2.

- Being understood by the therapist.
- Being accepted by the therapist.
- Having their problem be taken seriously by the therapist.
- The therapist not being shocked by the problem.

Factors relating to understanding

These factors are related to the views domain of the working alliance discussed in Chapter 3.

- Understanding what one can change and what one can't change.
- Finding the framework offered by the therapist to understand their problem useful.
- Finding the framework offered by the therapist to address their problem helpful.

- Seeing that one has a choice of holding a rigid attitude or a flexible attitude.
- Understanding the factors that one has been using to deal with the problem that, in fact, maintain the problem.

Factors relating to goals

These factors are related to the goals domain of the working alliance discussed in Chapter 4.

- Agreeing on a realistic and achievable goal with the therapist that concerns one's feelings and behaviours.
- Agreeing on a goal that helps the person deal constructively with the adversity.

Change factors

There are numerous change factors listed in the therapy literature. I think that the following may be particularly pertinent to VBTCs:

- Engaging emotionally in the conversation.
- Committing oneself to developing a flexible attitude and in particular to acting in ways that support the development of the flexible attitude.
- Choosing to face adversity and not to avoid it.
- Choosing to face internal experience and not to avoid it.
- Tolerating disturbed emotions and being willing to experience them.
- Tolerating discomfort in the service of one's goals.
- Tolerating problematic states such as uncertainty and lack of control.
- Accepting oneself as fallible.
- Accepting oneself for one's original problem.
- Accepting others as human.
- Accepting negative aspects of life.
- Putting matters into a broader perspective.
- Changing one's distorted inferences.
- Rehearsing new attitudes and/or new behaviours in the session.
- Changing behaviour.
- Being able to disclose one's problem in front of others.

- Hearing similar stories from others in the audience and getting a sense of universality.
- Being prepared to experiment with changing one's behaviour to elicit a healthier response in others.

As mentioned above, research needs to be done on VBTCs to see what volunteers find helpful about participating in these conversations.

Behaviours and action tendencies associated with unhealthy negative emotions and healthy negative emotions

Unhealthy negative emotions	Healthy negative emotions
Anxiety	**Concern**
• Avoid the threat • Withdraw physically from the threat • Ward off the threat (e.g. by rituals or superstitious behaviour) • Try to neutralise the threat (e.g. by being nice to people of whom one is afraid) • Distract self from the threat by engaging in other activity • Keep checking on the current status of the threat hoping to find that it has disappeared or become benign • Seek reassurance from others that the threat is benign • Seek support from others so that if the threat happens they will handle it or be there for rescue • Over-prepare in order to minimise the threat happening or so that one is prepared to meet it (NB it is the over-preparation that is the problem here)	• Face up to the threat without using any safety-seeking measures • Take constructive action to deal with the threat • Seek support from others to help self face up to the threat and then take independent constructive action rather than relying on them to handle it or be there for rescue • Prepare to meet the threat without over-preparation

Anxiety	Concern
• Tranquillise feelings so one doesn't think about the threat • Overcompensate for feeling vulnerable by seeking out an even greater threat to prove to self that one can cope	

Depression	Sadness
• Become overly dependent on and seek to cling to others (particularly in sociotropic depression) • Bemoan one's fate or that of others to anyone who will listen (particularly in pity-based depression) • Create an environment consistent with depressed feelings • Attempt to terminate feelings of depression in self-destructive ways • Either push away attempts to comfort one (in autonomous depression) or use such comfort to reinforce dependency (in sociotropic depression) or self- or other-pity (in pity-based depression)	• Seek out reinforcements after a period of mourning (particularly when inferential theme is loss) • Create an environment inconsistent with depressed feelings • Express feelings about the loss, failure or undeserved plight and talk in a non-complaining way about these feelings to significant others • Allow self to be comforted in a way that helps to express feelings of sadness and to mourn loss

Guilt	Remorse
• Escape from the unhealthy pain of guilt in self-defeating ways • Beg forgiveness from the person wronged • Promise unrealistically not to 'sin' again • Punish self physically or by deprivation • Defensively disclaim responsibility for wrongdoing • Make excuses for behaviour • Reject offers of forgiveness	• Face up to the healthy pain that accompanies the realisation that one has sinned • Ask, but do not beg, for forgiveness • Understand the reasons for wrongdoing and act on understanding • Atone for the sin by taking a penalty • Make appropriate amends • Do not make excuses for behaviour or enact other defensive behaviour • Accept offers of forgiveness

Shame	Disappointment
• Remove self from the 'gaze' of others • Isolate self from others • Save face by attacking other(s) for their 'shaming' behaviour • Defend threatened self-esteem in self-defeating ways • Ignore attempts by others to restore social equilibrium	• Continue to participate actively in social interaction • Respond positively to attempts of others to restore social equilibrium

Hurt	Sorrow
• Stop communicating with the other person • Sulk and make obvious hurt feelings without disclosing details of the matter • Indirectly criticise or punish the other person for their offence • Tell others how badly one has been treated, but don't take responsibility for any contribution to this	• Communicate your feelings to the other directly • Request, but do not demand, that the other person acts in a fairer manner • Discuss the situation with others in a balanced way, focusing on the way one has been treated and taking responsibility for any contribution one may have made to this

Unhealthy anger	Healthy anger
• Attack the other(s) physically, verbally or passive-aggressively • Displace the attack onto another person, animal or object • Withdraw aggressively • Recruit allies against the other(s)	• Self-assertion with the other(s) • Request, but do not demand, behavioural change from the other(s) • Leave an unsatisfactory situation non-aggressively after taking steps to deal with it

Unhealthy jealousy	Concern for one's relationship/healthy jealousy
• Seek constant reassurance that one is loved • Monitor the actions and feelings of partner • Search for evidence that partner is involved with someone else	• Allow partner to initiate expressing love without prompting them or seeking reassurance once they have done so

Unhealthy jealousy	Concern for one's relationship/healthy jealousy
• Attempt to restrict the movements or activities of partner • Set tests that partner has to pass • Retaliate for partner's presumed infidelity • Sulk	• Allow partner freedom without monitoring their feelings, actions and whereabouts • Allow partner to show natural interest in members of the opposite (or same) sex without setting tests • Communicate concern for your relationship in an open and non-blaming manner

Unhealthy envy	Healthy envy
• Disparage verbally the person who has the desired possession to others • Disparage verbally the desired possession to others • If possible, take away the desired possession from the other (either so that one will have it or that the other is deprived of it) • If possible, spoil or destroy the desired possession so that the other person does not have it	• Strive to obtain the desired possession if it is truly wanted

References

Bannister, D. & Fransella, F. (1986). *Inquiring Man: The Psychology of Personal Constructs*. London: Croom-Helm.

Barber, J. (1990). Miracle cures? Therapeutic consequences of clinical demonstrations. In J.K. Zeig & S.G. Gilligan (Eds), *Brief Therapy: Myths, Methods and Metaphors* (pp. 437–442). New York: Brunner-Mazel.

Beck, A.T. (1976). *Cognitive Therapy and the Emotional Disorders*. New York: International Universities Press.

Bloom, B.L. (1981). Focused single session therapy: Initial development and evaluation. In S.H. Budman (Ed.), *Forms of Brief Therapy* (pp. 167–216). New York: Guilford Press.

Bloom, B.L. (1992). *Planned Short-Term Psychotherapy: A Clinical Handbook*. Boston: Allyn & Bacon.

Bordin, E.S. (1979). The generalizability of the psychoanalytic concept of the working alliance. *Psychotherapy: Theory, Research and Practice*, *16*, 252–260.

Colman, A. (2015) *Oxford Dictionary of Psychology*. 4th Edition. Oxford: Oxford University Press.

Cooper, M. & Dryden, W. (Eds). (2016). *The Handbook of Pluralistic Counselling and Psychotherapy*. London: Sage.

Cooper, M. & McLeod, J. (2011). *Pluralistic Counselling and Psychotherapy*. London: Sage.

Covey, S.R. (1989). *The 7 Habits of Highly Effective People: Powerful Lessons in Personal Change*. New York: Simon & Schuster.

Dryden, W. (1995). *Brief Rational Emotive Behaviour Therapy*. Chichester: John Wiley & Sons.

Dryden, W. (1999). *How to Accept Yourself*. London: Sheldon.

Dryden, W. (2000). *Overcoming Procrastination*. London: Sheldon.

Dryden, W. (Ed.) (2002). *Idiosyncratic Rational Emotive Behaviour Therapy*. Ross-on-Wye: PCCS Books.

Dryden, W. (2006). *Counselling in a Nutshell*. London: Sage.

Dryden, W. (2011). *Counselling in a Nutshell*. 2nd Edition. London: Sage.

Dryden, W. (2012a). Rational emotive behaviour therapy (REBT). In W. Dryden (Ed.), *Cognitive Behaviour Therapies* (pp. 189–215). London: Sage.

Dryden, W. (Ed.) (2012b). *Cognitive Behaviour Therapies*. London: Sage.

Dryden, W. (2015). *Rational Emotive Behaviour Therapy: Distinctive Features*. 2nd Edition. Hove: Routledge.

Dryden, W. (2016). *When Time Is At a Premium: Cognitive-Behavioural Approaches to Single-Session Therapy and Very Brief Coaching*. London: Rationality Publications.

Dryden, W. (2017a). *Single-Session Integrated CBT (SSI-CBT): Distinctive Features*. Abingdon: Routledge.

Dryden, W. (2017b). *Very Brief Cognitive-Behavioural Coaching (VBCBC)*. Abingdon: Routledge.

Dryden, W. (2017c). *The Coaching Alliance: Theory and Guidelines for Practice*. Abingdon: Routledge.

Dryden, W. (2018). *Flexibility-Based Cognitive Behaviour Therapy: Practical Insights from 40 Years of Practice*. Abingdon: Routledge.

Dryden, W. & Ellis, A. (2003). *Albert Ellis Live!* London: Sage.

Ellis, A. (1963). Toward a more precise definition of 'emotional' and 'intellectual' insight. *Psychological Reports*, *13*, 125–126.

Ellis, A. (2005). *The Myth of Self-Esteem*. Amherst: Prometheus.

Ellis, A. (2007). *All Out! An Autobiography*. Amherst: Prometheus.

Ellis, A. & Joffe, D. (2002). A study of volunteer clients who experienced live sessions of rational emotive behavior therapy in front of a public audience. *Journal of Rational-Emotive & Cognitive-Behavior Therapy*, *20*, 151–158.

Harris, R. (2009). *An ACT Primer: An Easy-to-Read on Acceptance and Commitment Therapy*. Oakland: New Harbinger Publications.

Hayes, S.C., Strosahl, K.D. & Wilson, K.G. (2012). *Acceptance and Commitment Therapy: The Process and Practice of Mindful Change*. 2nd Edition. New York: Guilford.

Hedges, F. (2005). *An Introduction to Systemic Therapy with Individuals*. Basingstoke: Palgrave.

Hoyt, M.F. (Ed.) (1998). *The Handbook of Constructive Therapies: Innovative Approaches from Leading Practitioners*. San Francisco: Jossey-Bass.

Hoyt, M.F., Bobele, M., Slive, A., Young, J. & Talmon, M. (Eds) (2018). *Single-Session Therapy by Walk-In or Appointment: Administrative, Clinical, and Supervisory Aspects of One-at-a-Time Services*. New York: Routledge.

Hoyt, M.F. & Talmon, M. (Eds) (2014a). *Capturing the Moment: Single Session Therapy and Walk-In Services*. Bethel: Crown House Publishing Ltd.

Hoyt, M.F. & Talmon, M. (2014b). Editors' introduction: Single session therapy and walk-in services. In M.F. Hoyt & M. Talmon, M. (Eds), *Capturing the Moment: Single Session Therapy and Walk-In Services* (pp. 1–26). Bethel: Crown House Publishing Ltd.

Jones-Smith, E. (2014). *Strengths-Based Therapy: Connecting Theory, Practice, and Skills.* Thousand Oaks: Sage.

Keller, G. & Papasan, J. (2012) *The One Thing: The Surprisingly Simple Truth behind Extraordinary Results.* Austin: Bard Press.

Kellogg, S. (2015) *Transformational Chairwork: Using Psychotherapeutic Dialogues in Clinical Practice.* Lanham: Rowman & Littlefield.

Lazarus, A.A. (1993). Tailoring the therapeutic relationship, or being an authentic chameleon. *Psychotherapy: Theory, Research & Practice, 30,* 404–407.

Lipchik, E. (1994). The rush to be brief. *The Family Therapy Networker, 18,* 34–39.

McLeod, J. (1997). *Narrative and Psychotherapy.* London: Sage.

Maultsby, M.C. Jr. (1984). *Rational Behaviour Therapy.* Englewood Cliffs: Prentice-Hall.

Talmon, M. (1990). *Single Session Therapy: Maximising the Effect of the First (and Often Only) Therapeutic Encounter.* San Francisco: Jossey-Bass.

Talmon, M., Hoyt, M.F. & Rosenbaum, R. (1988). When the first session is the last: A map for rapid therapeutic change. Short course presented at the Third Congress of Ericksonian Hypnosis and Psychotherapy, San Francisco, December, 1988. The Milton H. Erickson Foundation, Phoenix, AZ.

Ratner, H., George, E. & Iveson, C. (2012). *Solution Focused Brief Therapy: 100 Key Points and Techniques.* Hove, Routledge.

Rogers, C.R. (1957). The necessary and sufficient conditions of therapeutic personality change. *Journal of Consulting Psychology, 21,* 95–103.

Rosenbaum, R., Hoyt, M.F. & Talmon, M. (1990). The challenge of single-session therapies: Creating pivotal moments. In R.A. Wells & V.J. Giannetti (Eds), *Handbook of the Brief Psychotherapies* (pp. 165–189). New York: Plenum Press.

Index